UNION-OCCUPIED
MARYLAND

CLAUDIA FLOYD

UNION-OCCUPIED MARYLAND

A Civil War Chronicle of
CIVILIANS & SOLDIERS

Charleston · London

THE
History
PRESS

Published by The History Press
Charleston, SC 29403
www.historypress.net

Cover photo courtesy of Dr. Dean Herrin (National Park Service) and Princeton University
Library. From *Frank Leslie's Illustrated Newspaper.*

First published 2014

Manufactured in the United States

ISBN 978.1.62619.611.7

Library of Congress CIP data applied for.

Contents

Acknowledgements

I would like to extend my most heartfelt gratitude to Gail Stephens for her very insightful and valuable recommendations and to Peter Olson for helping in every way possible and for being a husband extraordinaire.

Cumberland

Hagerstown

South Mountain
Antietam

Maryland Physiography
&
Civil War Sites

City or Town	O
State Capital	☆
Battlefield Site	X
B&O Railroad	---

Maryland map. *Base map courtesy of Raymond E. Sterner.*

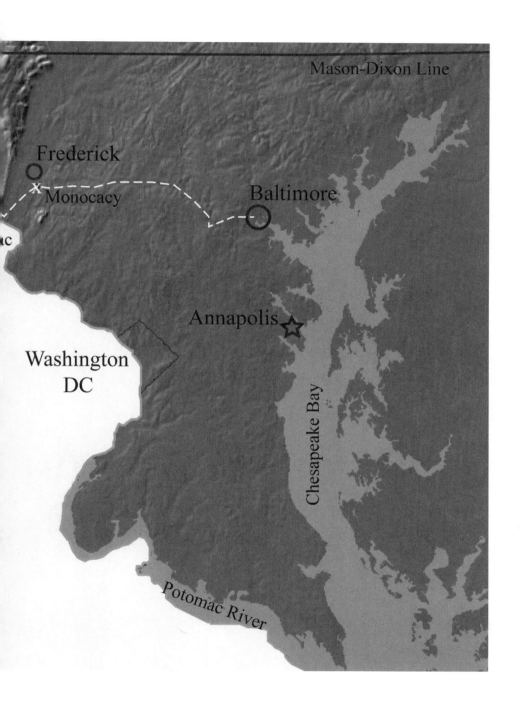

Mason-Dixon Line

Frederick

Monocacy

Baltimore

Annapolis

Washington
DC

Chesapeake Bay

Potomac River

ac

Introduction

When sorrows come,
they come not single spies,
but in battalions.
—Shakespeare, Hamlet

The Hagerstown, Maryland newspaper *Herald of Freedom and Torch Light* discoursed eloquently on the benefits of the presence of the Union army in its June 26, 1861 issue: "Here the soldiers and the citizens, when the former are off duty, hold fellowship with each other, and mutually contribute to each other's comfort and convenience and to the good order of society generally. This is the protection which the Federal Army extends to every law abiding community." The editors contrasted this with the behavior of the rebels that consisted of "driving loyal men from their homes, hunting them down like wild beasts, and confiscating or carrying off their property."[1] These remarks in a unionist newspaper reflected an idyllic period that did not last long in Hagerstown or anywhere else in the state. While the Union soldiers provided many benefits to the community at large, there was a darker side of their occupation that has not received sufficient attention in the literature on the Civil War.

Because Maryland was the home to an influential, geographically dispersed and activist secessionist minority, the soldiers became both symbols of and enforcers of stringent procedures designed to retain control over the population. The military's attempt to tightly restrict the behavior of the

Southern supporters was coupled with the necessity to maintain discipline and order within its own ranks. In addition, the occupation was designed both to deter and to defend against Confederate intrusions into what was a largely loyal border state. The fact that the Union army was unable to address successfully all three of these commitments created an environment of risk for Maryland's civilians. In the Civil War, state residents were exposed to numerous fighting engagements, to errant and unlawful behavior by soldiers on both sides and to the overzealous actions against backers of the South by the authorities. All of these factors were complicated by the upheaval of war that unleashed a revolution in race relations, deeply affecting both blacks and whites in what remained a slave state until November 1864.

The American Civil War was characterized by an unprecedented degree of social connectivity between civilians and their citizen soldiers. Between 1861 and 1865, approximately 10 percent of the total population of the United States (3.2 million out of 32 million) served in the military, compared to about .45 percent in today's all-volunteer armed forces.[2] A majority of Americans during the Civil War had family, friends or neighbors fighting on one side or the other. This psychological bond was accompanied by proximity to the soldiers who came as protectors, liberators or conquerors, depending on one's partisan perspective. In Maryland, the Union occupation was concentrated in its major cities and towns (Baltimore, Annapolis, Frederick, Hagerstown and Cumberland) and along its railroads, particularly the B&O, a circumstance that resulted in regular contact between citizens and soldiers. While the majority of the men customarily conducted themselves in a manner that was a credit to their uniform, the army contained undisciplined individuals who created an array of problems for local residents. The general orders issued by the offices of the provost marshal throughout the state reflected the concern and frustration of the military authorities, who witnessed an escalating number of episodes of drunk and disorderly conduct, affrays and property destruction by the men in blue. Local newspapers regularly featured items on the military's involvement in major and minor crimes ranging from assaults to shootings and stabbings, often with civilians as victims. In addition, residents learned to fear for the safety of their children, as soldiers sped recklessly through the streets on their horses and at times accidently discharged their weapons, injuring the unsuspecting victims of inebriated, careless or inexperienced men.

The Union occupation brought into the state and along its transportation corridors a highly transient population of disproportionately young males who lacked ties to the local community and were armed and trained to

Civilians in camp. *Library of Congress.*

fight. High testosterone levels, the tedium of camp, a new and enticing environment and the lure of alcohol created a volatile mixture that military authorities sought to control but did not always succeed in doing so. As Private Alfred Roe observed: "The spirit of deviltry often prompts men and boys, especially the latter, to do unaccountable things."[3] Soldiers guilty of violating the Articles of War or the criminal codes filled the civilian and military jails in the cities, led to the establishment of military commissions heavily backlogged with cases and induced fear and anger in some Maryland residents.

Greedy and unprincipled civilians, designated "enablers" here, developed methods of taking advantage of their Union occupiers. Forbidden to sell

Drummer boys in camp. *Library of Congress.*

alcohol to soldiers, many owners of bars, groggeries and brothels ignored military orders and catered to the weaknesses of the men. Successively stricter regulations and more stringent punishments did not succeed in stopping this traffic in alcohol or sex at any time during the war. Citizens also assisted in hiding and abetting deserters and even providing them with civilian clothing in order to escape. Dishonorable individuals, often women, used drugs, sex or deception to steal from and cheat soldiers when they were asleep, sick, wounded or simply not paying attention. Men in camps in and around cities were especially susceptible to the lures of these enablers because of boredom and the closeness of myriad enticements. As Lieutenant Colonel Wilder Dwight explained from Camp Hicks, near Frederick, he was very busy with court-martial work, "punishing all the peccadilloes of the march, and the indiscretions consequent upon a sudden exposure to the temptations of civilization and enlightenment—to wit, whiskey."[4]

While the troublesome soldiers and their civilian enablers developed a symbiotic relationship, the majority of citizens were simply concerned with maintaining as much of their routine as possible in the midst of the war. The unionists saw the soldiers as the guardians of their liberty and property from the enemy just across the Potomac River. This image of the Union occupiers as protectors was gradually weakened by their inability to defend many Marylanders from the ravages of three successive Confederate invasions in 1862, 1863 and 1864. In the latter year, Lieutenant General Jubal Early's men reached the outskirts of both Baltimore and the nation's capital. In addition to these major invasions, partisans regularly crossed the Potomac, tearing up railroad tracks, vandalizing the C&O Canal and pillaging farms and stores in the southern and western parts of Maryland. In the skirmishes that occurred in the state and in the Battles of South Mountain, Antietam and Monocacy, the Union soldiers posed as much of a threat to civilians and their property as did the Confederates.

The corridor of land from Baltimore to Cumberland was crossed and re-crossed so many times during the war that residents became very accustomed to the sights and sounds of the military in motion. In Baltimore, because it was a critical railroad hub, a staggering 800,000 Federal soldiers passed through the Union Relief Association rooms even before the war reached its third year.[5] The Confederates also came, but in waves rather than in large steady accretions. When General Robert E. Lee's army first invaded Maryland in 1862, Charles A. Tenney, of the Seventh Ohio Regiment, remarked in a letter to his sweetheart that they never dreamed that they would end up fighting in a loyal state, "yet the deed was accomplished, and even Fredericktown a union city was invested and *infested* by a subtle and cunning foe."[6] Less than a year later, children, who were sitting on a porch watching a regiment in the Gettysburg campaign march by their Maryland house, greeted the men with lusty cheers for Jefferson Davis until their mother saw the bluecoats and warned the children to hush, and so they began to shout, "Hurrah for the Union!"[7] Private Alfred S. Roe, of the Ninth New York Heavy Artillery, observed the reaction of the citizens to the turnover in the possession of Frederick in the third Confederate invasion: "Flags were numerous as we proceeded through the streets…A few hours afterwards rebel banners were as common as were now Union flags…It would seem that the good citizens learned wisdom and were prepared to placate either army."[8] State residents, even the very young, were compelled to adapt quickly, but the rumors, fear and apprehension accompanying the shifting fortunes of war were challenging for all civilians.

Marylanders also confronted a major transformation of their socioeconomic system as "the peculiar institution" of human bondage was gradually undermined. Secessionist owners of slaves perceived the military's decision to employ African American troops in 1863 as a threat

The Fourth
USCT Infantry.
*Library of
Congress.*

to their "property" rights, when zealous recruiters cruised along the shores of the Chesapeake Bay, up the tidal rivers of the Eastern Shore and on the streets of Frederick to pick up new enlistees. After much outrage and many complaints about this practice, the War Department implemented procedures for compensating loyal slaveholders for their loss, but such was not the case for Southern supporters. While militarily expedient, not all soldiers or citizens endorsed either liberating the slaves or arming individuals previously prohibited from possessing weapons. Tensions were often aggravated when Maryland's whites witnessed United States Colored Troops (USCT) in uniform, a sight that some found offensive to their sense of racial superiority and to their belief that blacks were lacking in the skills and courage requisite for combat. While some soldiers agreed with Abraham Lincoln's desire to free those in bondage and enable them to contribute to the war effort, others resented this empowerment. White soldiers were implicated in racial episodes, including violence, directed against both black civilians and United States Colored Troops during and right after the Civil War. According to Bell Wiley, as the Federals increasingly perceived the life of the soldier as dreary and miserable, they looked around for an outlet "to heap on it their accumulated displeasure." Since blacks were strongly identified with the conflict, they "became scapegoats on whom the soldier could spill his hatred for the war."[9]

Also in peril were those secessionists who decided to aid the Southern cause through activities such as smuggling, spying or sabotage. Employing words, deeds or symbols of support for the Confederacy were acts defined as treason and punishable as such. Those captured faced possible imprisonment, house arrest, confiscation of property, exile or even execution. Unionists were encouraged by the military to report on the treasonous utterances or behaviors of their neighbors, a practice that became so prevalent in Baltimore that Major General John Wool had to issue special orders to ensure that mere revenge or mischief were not the motives. The divisiveness engendered by this practice of establishing spies and informers was pronounced and served only to exacerbate the alienation and poisonous atmosphere already apparent between partisans of both sides. While the Union employed spies throughout Maryland, with forty to fifty male and female detectives in Baltimore City alone, under the occupation, every soldier or citizen in the neighborhood was potentially an informer.[10]

The relationship between civilians and soldiers in Maryland in the Civil War was both complex and dynamic. Both parties had unrealistic expectations: the Union forces in terms of their capability of protecting

Maryland Confederate cavalryman. State residents fought on both sides. *Library of Congress.*

loyal citizens in the border states from exposure to the hazards and privations of war and the civilians for their failure to fully grasp the forces that at times produced errant soldiers who pillaged, abused alcohol, committed crimes and deserted the cause for which they had originally fought. The invincible, courageous hero, dashing and daring, delivering glorious victories to a grateful populace, was the substance of romantic novels, history textbooks and Independence Day parades, but it depicted only one side of the actualities of four years of grueling civil war. The turmoil and trauma entailed in this conflict were unprecedented in our history and transformative both for the soldiers and for the citizens, who were either their supporters or their critics.

This examination of the letters, journals, memoirs, regimental histories and official records of the Civil War clearly indicates that despite the potential perils of an occupational force, most Maryland residents accepted the Union soldiers and sustained them throughout the Civil War. To the majority, the men in blue were "*our* soldiers," even when crushing Federal defeats at sites like Manassas, Fredericksburg and Chancellorsville taxed the spirits of all but the most diehard supporters. The resolution of the Union authorities and the military to prevail, whatever the price to be paid, was matched by most Maryland civilians, who came to accept the misconduct of a minority of rogue soldiers and consequences of the military presence on their lives as part and parcel of the sacrifices required in modern warfare.

1

Militarization of Maryland

*In fact, with the artillery posted here, Baltimore itself could be laid in ashes,
should the occasion require it.*[11]
—*Alfred Davenport*

On June 8, 1861, the Eleventh Regiment of Indiana Zouaves, rough-looking men bedecked in their strange and colorful uniforms, arrived in Cumberland and immediately established a camp on Rose Hill overlooking a city nestled in the folds of the western Maryland mountains. As local resident and later historian Will Lowdermilk remarked, "They seemed to have fallen from the clouds." While the soldiers restored a sense of normalcy to a town that had been rife with panic, insecurity and rumors, they brought with them a military culture alien to most residents. It did not take long before the Union authorities started regulating the tempo of daily life. "Free speech was no longer allowed. Secession sentiments were banned. Informers became busy. Citizens were arrested and marched under guard to the camp, and having received a lecture on loyalty…were tendered the oath of allegiance and then permitted to return home."[12] The number of troops in Cumberland and elsewhere in the state fluctuated throughout the war, but the militarization of life was only just beginning in the spring of 1861.

The transient nature of the population in Maryland during the Civil War was a major source of social upheaval. Frequent rotation of military units, transportation of wounded, the relocation of Confederate prisoners

Union soldier with two women. *Library of Congress.*

of war and the flight of refugees from Virginia's devastated lands all strained the resources and patience of Maryland residents. Baltimore, the nation's third-largest city at the time, was a hub for much of the activity because of its size, location and railroad connections. Sir William Howard Russell, on his travels through Maryland in 1861, noticed that from Havre de Grace southward to the nation's capital, "the stations on the rail were guarded by soldiers, as though the enemy were expected to destroy the bridges and tear up the rails…Sentinels are posted, pickets thrown out, and in the open fields by the wayside troops are seen to be moving, as though the battle was close at hand."[13] From Baltimore to Annapolis in particular, the rail cars were packed with soldiers on the move, passing through guard posts and camps all along the way. There were "huts and tents, huts of pine boughs, huts of logs, of sods, of rails, every conceivable kind of shelter for the eternal soldier." The correspondent who observed this in November 1861 noted, "Over ten thousand soldiers lie that night within a mile of Annapolis."[14]

The militarization of Maryland was very difficult for the average citizen to put out of mind, particularly with the incessant movement of men and supplies via the transportation network. In Frederick, the streets were constantly busy with the steady passage of up to one hundred mule teams going by each day, many with hay or other items, or just empty. Civilians in Baltimore and surrounding areas witnessed a steady stream of sheep, hogs and cattle in transit to the District of Columbia for the army.[15] Two hundred turkeys driven from Pennsylvania to the nation's capital had to be diverted from the main street of Middletown because soldiers under Major General Banks were marching through there.[16] Jesse Dixon of Urbana, who was just a boy when the Civil War began, remembered the passage of the army trains going by his house that could be heard for miles. He said that the long lines of supply wagons continually came, "lumbering by till our ears were fairly deafened as they rattled over the ungraded roads, freighted heavily on unspringed wagon-beds."[17] The rhythm of everyday life, particularly in Maryland's farming countryside, was transformed by the needs of the vast military machine.

In Baltimore, in the first year of the war, a record number of fortifications were under construction, with the city eventually protected by "44 forts, batteries, redoubts, and armed camps and about 20 unarmed camps."[18] Those erected on Federal Hill overlooking the harbor were particularly imposing because some of the guns were aimed at the heart of the city, designed to maintain order within, as well as to protect from any Confederate attack from the outside. Stephen H. Bogardus, of the Fifth New York Duryee Zouaves, stationed at Camp Federal Hill, recorded in his journal on October 8, 1861, "We are mounting the guns daily, and we expect soon to have 64 guns mounted, all of them 42 lb. Columbiads. They will command the whole city of Baltimore and the adjacent territory." He observed that with this power, "we can disperse any crowd of disputants in the city."[19]

Pratt Street Riot
in Baltimore. *Frank
Leslie's Illustrated
Newspaper.*

This military capacity plus the regular arrests of Maryland secessionists were steps designed to be threatening and to serve as deterrents to any further disorders following the Pratt Street Riot on April 19, 1861. This violent event, involving a confrontation between the Sixth Massachusetts Regiment and Baltimore citizens, resulted in twelve deaths, with twenty-four soldiers and an unknown number of civilians injured. Determined to show the disloyal residents that they would not tolerate any more hostile actions, the soldiers of the Seventeenth Massachusetts conducted drills and other demonstrations of their power in the streets.[20] When some Southern sympathizers were arrested in 1862 and Union military authorities feared another riot as a result, troops around Baltimore were told to be in a state of readiness. When all remained quiet, a soldier at nearby Camp Millington concluded, "I guess there is no danger, as they are pretty well afraid of our forts, which surround them."[21] Melville Hayward, of the Seventh New York National Guard, also implied that the military was an intimidating presence in a letter to his aunt. Asserting that Baltimore was a seething volcano because of secessionist unrest, he observed, "On the Fourth of July we fired salute from our heavy guns and reverberations through the city must have made the secesh tremble."[22]

On the Eastern Shore, in Annapolis and in western Maryland, other military installations and camps, both temporary and permanent, were established as the Union enhanced its presence in the state. To some Marylanders, the thrill, novelty and pageantry that accompanied the soldiers' arrival were irresistible attractions. The *Baltimore American and Daily Advertiser* estimated that on May 17, 1861, nearly twenty thousand residents visited the Union troops bivouacked on a hill near Fort McHenry, hoping to watch the nightly drills and dress parades. While most were supportive of the soldiers or at least tolerated their presence, trouble between the military and civilians was apparent even at this early date in the war. John F. Thompson, a merchant tailor from South Gay Street, told a group of Federals that they should go to Harpers Ferry, where they could meet a real foe. A soldier and his wife who accompanied him both assaulted Thompson for his words, an omen of further trouble to follow. By the end of May 1861, one of the city's newspapers commented on the restlessness and lack of discipline of the men of the Twenty-second Pennsylvania Volunteers at Fort Patterson: "A disorderly spirit has in a number of cases been exhibited by some members of this Regiment, who have, while intoxicated, conducted themselves in such a manner that the citizens of East Baltimore would be much gratified if the Regiment was transferred to some other place."[23]

It was apparent, even in the first year of the Union occupation, that soldiers had a culture and code of conduct very dissimilar from those of civilians. Accidents, misunderstandings and incidents that escalated into violence resulted from these differences. Silas Hines of Rohrersville was shot by a Union picket for his refusal to halt when commanded, possibly because of his failure to understand military procedures or simply due to the fact that he did not hear the order. The *Herald of Freedom and Torch Light* observed, "None but the most sober and reliable should be assigned to posts of such importance in the heart of a populous county such as Washington." In Baltimore, as the eight hundred members of the Twenty-second New York Regiment came into Camden Station, one soldier stumbled, his musket discharged and he killed another. The men then started shooting wildly into the ceiling of the depot, and the Minié balls passed through the roof, injuring two civilians, resulting in one amputation. At nearby Camp Carroll, a ceremonial firing to honor departing soldiers resulted in an accident in which a Mrs. Hambleton was struck by a musket ball half a mile away. Luckily for the woman, the ball hit the pit of her stomach, "but meeting resistance by a busque, and some whalebone, the missile rebounded and fell to the pavement, only inflicting a painful sensation."[24] Hannah Loftus, a young girl who lived on Falls Road, was not so fortunate. She died instantly from a bullet through the forehead in an accident caused by Private Lewis Chapman, from a Maryland regiment, who was home on a furlough.[25] Incidents such as these became increasingly common with the proliferation of guns in the hands of those who did not exercise caution for the civilians who resided in their midst.

For Maryland's children, the arrival of the soldiers with all their accoutrements was both a memorable and thrilling experience. For Jesse Dixon, a ten-year-old boy from Urbana when the war began, it was a special opportunity to observe the activity in camps near his home and to collect souvenirs. He recollected that when the bugle calls rang for the soldiers to gather around the commander's tent, even the horses dropped what they were doing and assembled in back of the soldiers.[26] For Benjamin Deffinbaugh and his sister Emily, the war was a chance to outwit the soldiers who frequently came to their farm in the Cumberland area. One morning, when their parents were away, the marauders of the First New York Cavalry rode up and asked the children to blow their conch shell, used as a dinner bell, if anyone came by. As the soldiers started to shoot their chickens, Emily blew the conch loudly. The frightened men jumped on their horses and soon disappeared.[27]

Two soldiers with civilians. *Library of Congress.*

But for a number of children, the militarization of Maryland added an unfortunate and at times tragic dimension to their young lives. With their natural inclination to imitate the soldiers, it was common to see the children "playing war." Such was the case with two boys in Baltimore, of the ages seven and eight, who were playing with a gun when they got into a fight, and one shot the other in the leg.[28] Two children of Joseph Palmer, who lived on a farm in Tilghmanton, "borrowed" the musket of a Federal who was sleeping in their barn. When another soldier walked in and told them to drop the gun, it accidently discharged, killing two people.[29] In Baltimore, where kids noticed the military feverishly erecting fortifications around the city, they decided to do the same. When they started to impress other children walking by to do some of the construction work on the fort for them, a fight with bricks broke out, and chaos ensued until a policeman broke up the fracas.[30]

Some children lost family members in the fighting, and some were witnesses to the most fearful and horrid dimensions of warfare. A little

Soldier and a child in Zouave uniform. *Library of Congress.*

boy by the name of Charles Wilson Bingham lived on his family farm at the western edge of South Mountain. His fifteen-year-old brother escaped out of the bedroom window and was suspected of joining the army with some of his friends. Bub, as Charles was called as a boy, remembered going to Antietam soon after the battle and watching his sobbing mother inspect the fresh mounds of earth, looking for his brother, but no one had information on the boy's whereabouts.[31] The *Frederick Examiner* carried a story of a young girl, studying at a convent in town, who was wearing a Confederate flag on her breast and parading up and down outside on the streets in town singing, "Maryland, My Maryland." The mother superior grabbed the flag, threw it on the ground, stomped on it and angrily scolded the girl. Two of her brothers, Confederate POWs, were escorted through Frederick the next day and told her that her father had been killed in battle in Virginia the day before. The girl started screaming, shrieking and weeping so hard that she went into convulsions. The surgeons in the hospital declared that she was in critical condition and probably would not recover.[32] It was clear even early in the Civil War that the conflict was merciless and could touch the lives of anyone in the civilian population, including its very youngest members.

When Union authorities began the occupation of Maryland, the commanders issued orders designed to facilitate a positive working relationship with the civilian population. Brigadier General Benjamin Butler, when his troops took possession of Baltimore City on May 15, 1861, dispensed the following order: "Any infraction of the laws by the troops under his command, or any disorderly or unsoldierlike conduct, or any interference with private property, he desires to have immediately reported to him…and if any soldier so far forgets himself as to break these laws…*he shall be most rigorously punished*."[33] Two days later, Butler, who had not been officially authorized to occupy the state's largest city, was relieved of command. The *Baltimore American and Commercial Advertiser* editorialized on his transfer to Fortress Monroe by expressing gratification. "The extreme views and arbitrary action of General Butler were offensive to the loyal citizens of Baltimore."[34] For the secessionists, occupation under any commander or under any conditions was unacceptable, as the newspaper the *South* made clear:

> *They have seized the Capital of the State and converted it into a military depot; they have seized the railroads and converted them into military roads; they have seized our steamboats and converted them into military transports.*

They have established over us and among us a Military despotism of the most absolute and repressive character.[35]

This militarization in Maryland transformed the lives of nearly every resident by 1865—young and old, men and women, secessionists and unionists, free blacks and slaves.

As the course of the war progressed, both citizens and soldiers were forced to adjust to an increasingly burdensome environment. When Lincoln signed the first federal draft law in March 1863, all males between eighteen and forty-five were compelled to enroll. Those evading the draft left the state, hired substitutes or even became bounty jumpers. All this manpower was expensive. Residents in some jurisdictions were subject to a "bounty tax" to entice men into the Union army by offering larger bonuses for enlistment. Those with higher incomes were compelled to pay the nation's federal income tax. Civilians had to contend with restrictions on their travel across the Potomac, and later, passes were required for westward journeys beyond Monocacy Junction near Frederick. When martial law was declared, as was the case in Baltimore after the Pratt Street Riot and later, during the Gettysburg campaign, in Annapolis in July 1864 and in Frederick in response to the draft, the restrictions on business, travel and socializing were even more onerous. Some cities and towns in Maryland were overwhelmed with numbers of soldiers that at times exceeded their total antebellum population. Many civilians in their journals and letters remarked on the problem of wartime inflation with the increased demand. As the *Herald* observed, "In consequence of the immense accession of soldiers and other strangers in our population, the prices of everything which enters into the consumption of a family have greatly advanced."[36]

The presence of the Federal army also had implications for Maryland politics. Soldiers and unionists supported one another against those who opposed the Lincoln administration or belonged to the Democratic Party. After the early arrests in 1861 of Maryland's secessionist leaders, newspaper editors and Baltimore's mayor and police commissioners, Union Party members of various factions (conservative and Unconditional) dominated Maryland state and local politics until the war terminated. These Unionists instituted an oath requirement in 1862 in order to be employed by the government in Baltimore or to teach in its schools. The military cooperated with local governments at election time, not just to maintain order, but also to ensure that those who were judged disloyal did not have the opportunity to exercise the franchise. Soldiers interfered with elections in some locations by requiring an oath of allegiance or simply appearing and menacing voters. When Major General John D. Dix was in command of the Middle Department, he issued a proclamation to the U.S. marshal and to the provost marshal to arrest any disloyal citizens attempting to vote. They were to make an effort, Dix said, "to secure a free and fair expression of the voice of the people of Maryland and at the same time to prevent the ballot boxes from being polluted by treasonable votes."[37] In Cumberland in western Maryland, some citizens who had taken the oath of allegiance were prevented from voting on the 1864 Constitution because they refused to answer additional questions posed by election judges.

Sometimes they went too far. An order from Brigadier General Erastus B. Tyler, announced from his headquarters at the Northwestern Defense of Baltimore in November 1863, mandated that the men in his command were to cease their obstruction of meetings being held in various wards to nominate candidates for local office. Tyler noted, "This interference is made all the more aggravating from the fact that there were soldiers appearing with firearms outside their own wards and in such numbers as to intimidate and override the citizens whose rights we are here to protect."[38] The military continued at times to interfere in politics despite Tyler's order. This was the case on November 4, 1864, when soldiers were sent to disrupt and close down a mass meeting of Democrats in the city of Baltimore.[39]

Major General Lew Wallace, an astute politician in his own right, understood the importance of close ties between the military and the political elite. In a letter to Secretary of War Edwin Stanton in April 1864, Wallace asked that the Soldiers' Relief efforts be placed under his personal auspices to save money and so that he could use it as a "means to draw to my support and that of the union *cause* the active and practical sympathy of many of the wisest, purest and best of the Unionists in Baltimore."[40] The mutual reinforcement the Union Party and the military authorities offered each other provided the Middle Department with the latitude to exercise enormous control over the residents in the area. In addition, heavy censorship of the newspapers and other publications meant that the media of the day generally were a validating force for the existing civilian and military status quo during the Civil War.

The close cooperation between the military and the civilian government in Maryland extended to the state level. The General Assembly provided the authority to pursue the secessionists in the state with the passage of the Treason Act, which went into effect on April 15, 1862. According to the legislation, treason was defined as "to levy war against the State, to adhere

Union soldier. *Library of Congress.*

to its enemies or give them 'aid or comfort.'" It was made punishable "by death, or imprisonment in the penitentiary at the discretion of the court, for not less than six or more than twenty years."[41] This law resulted in the overcrowding of Fort McHenry and military jails with prisoners, a serious backlog of cases awaiting investigation by the provost marshal's office in Baltimore and the establishment of two military commissions by 1864, when the first was unable to handle all the cases expeditiously.

The Maryland judiciary was also affected by the presence of the Union army. The most famous casualty of this branch was the Honorable Richard B. Carmichael, a circuit court judge for Kent, Queen Anne's, Talbot and Caroline Counties on the Eastern Shore. Carmichael was a Confederate sympathizer and an outspoken opponent of the arbitrary arrests that were occurring in the state, a practice he perceived to be a violation of the Constitution. In May 1862, deputies, supported by 125 soldiers outside, descended on Carmichael's courtroom and arrested him in an incident that sparked a great deal of controversy. The deputies pulled out three pistols, struck the judge on the head with the barrels of their guns and dragged the blood-soaked man down from his platform and out the door.[42] He was placed in Fort McHenry and then moved to Fort Lafayette and was not released until December 1862. In a letter to William Price on June 3, 1862, George Vickers expressed his consternation at the actions taken leading to the imprisonment: "The community here have been shocked, by the outrage; every good citizen deems himself insulted, by the indignity offered to the Judge, and the desecration of the Temple of Justice."[43]

An interesting twist on the relationship between soldiers and citizens in Maryland was raised by Judge Hugh Bond of Baltimore when he sent a communication to judges on the Eastern Shore protesting the practice of permitting people to serve on juries who had not taken the oath of allegiance. The *Easton Gazette*, an Eastern Shore newspaper that was staunchly unionist, argued that nearly three hundred people on an adopted list in 1863 fell into the disloyal category, and the list even included some who had been sentenced to Fort Warren or indicted by a U.S. court. The *Gazette* maintained that this was very problematic because it was in the criminal courts where treason laws were enforced and where soldiers and officers of the Union army were liable to be tried.[44] The potential for secessionist citizens to sit in judgment on Federal troops was highly objectionable to many in Maryland.

While the Union army's occupation benefitted local merchants, spurred production in industries and shipbuilding and led to the awarding of contracts from commissaries of subsistence, it was also harsh, restrictive and intrusive at times. With divided loyalties in the state and a vigorous secessionist minority, the military never reached the point of fully trusting residents, particularly in southern Maryland and in Baltimore City. The latter had acquired a bold and unruly reputation early in the war that was never entirely eradicated. Union Secret Service agent LaFayette Baker said in this regard: "Of all the places north of Mason and Dixon's line, Baltimore had the preeminence in the early development of treason, and its defiant audacity. It is doubtful whether any other city furnished as largely and promptly for the rebel army the sons of aristocratic families."[45] While Baker misplaced Baltimore on the map, many Union officials shared his perspective on the city. The results of this distrust were that wagons were searched, warrantless arrests and seizures were frequent and detectives roamed the streets seeking traitors and "suspicious characters." The military's attempts to uncover and punish the secessionists in its midst were compromised and undermined at times by its inability to control all of its soldiers and officers.

2

Discipline in the Union Army

Every field yellow with wheat, and every house full of eatables. The army, however, sweeps down fences and grain, eats every mouthful and steals most of the horses.[46]
—Richard T. Auchmuty, Fifth Corps

Both the Union and Confederate armies experienced serious discipline problems throughout the Civil War. Insubordination, desertion, straggling, pillaging and other crimes have been the hallmarks of armies since the advent of recorded history, and this conflict was no exception. The citizen soldiers of the Civil War had one serious defect, according to Captain George F. Noyes, and that was "the want of proper discipline." This, he said, "greatly vitiates and impairs the fighting value of our citizen troops—a defect having its origin mainly in the method of their enlistment." Noyes explained that officers often went to school or lived near the men they were commanding, creating a situation where the officer was uncomfortable giving an order and the soldier was resentful in taking it.[47] According to a book written during the war on camp life, those officers who rigidly enforced regulations were dubbed "bigoted man killers" and were especially despised because rigor was not a strong component of the American soldier's character. Brought up in a free country and accustomed

Camp Carroll with a B&O train (at left) and Baltimore in the background. *Library of Congress.*

to self-sufficiency and equality, the distinctions in rank were especially odious to these men.[48] The Reverend Theodore Gerrish, a private from the Twentieth Maine, believed that it was particularly difficult for a Yankee to adapt to a soldier's life because his natural inquisitiveness led him to question why an order was given and his independence made it difficult to obey. He noted, "At home he considered himself as good as any other person, and in the army he failed to understand why a couple of gilt straps upon the shoulders of one who at home was far beneath him should there make him so much his superior."[49]

The incessant drills, marches and maneuvers of camp required enlistees to adjust quickly to a routine of strict regimentation. Away from the front and the sights and sounds of battle, the level of discipline often seemed unwarranted and harsh by those who had never been exposed to the demands of military service. Bored to death in Baltimore, some new inductees from Fort McHenry went down to the water's edge and decided to discharge their firearms at fishing boats in the Chesapeake Bay, some as far away as a mile offshore. Others, feeling trapped at nearby Fort Federal Hill, tunneled their way through the earth below to create an incline that would deliver them out onto Pratt Street near their favorite beer saloon and billiard hall.[50] While such antics appeared to be fairly common in training camps, many of these same men later realized the value of order, obedience and rigid discipline after they had been in battle.

The soldiers in the Civil War were exposed to many privations, including forced marches, inadequate or vile-tasting food, lack of sleep and unsanitary conditions. There were extended periods of time when they were not engaged, particularly in winter quarters or between campaigns, resulting in ennui and homesickness. Jacob Engelbrecht estimated that in December 1861 there were fifteen regiments located in or near Frederick with approximately fifteen thousand men thronging the town's streets.[51] John Mead Gould of the Tenth Maine Regiment went to Frederick at the end of January 1862 and observed: "The streets are full of idle soldiers, dirty soldiers, Zouaves, Gray-coated individuals, etc...The soldiers I passed were mostly dirty and ill-bred. They were in every shop door and lounging on every corner."[52] Failure to receive a pass from an officer sometimes fueled resentment and at times resulted in disgruntled soldiers sneaking out of camp or forging signatures of their officers, as sixteen-year-old Tom Hinds, of the First Maryland Cavalry, did with his friends in Baltimore.[53]

The patriotic enthusiasm and excitement that led men to enlist at the onset of the war diminished as it progressed, often replaced by such fundamental desires as survival and the avoidance of danger, hardship and discomfort. The disorder of war and the soldier's license to kill the enemy helped to weaken traditional ethical restraints on behavior. Some of the depredations associated with the Union forces in the Antietam campaign appeared "to have stemmed from a coarsening of values characteristic of veteran soldiers."[54] Several days after the battle, General in Chief Henry Halleck sent a message to Brigadier General George Stoneman in Poolesville stating, "It is also represented that the troops of your division are pillaging and plundering the country. Stringent measures must be resorted to enforce order."[55] This behavior by the Federals was even more shocking because it occurred in a state that remained in the Union and in a region where the population was predominantly loyal.

Pillaging was a serious problem in both armies, although in the Antietam campaign it appeared to a number of contemporary observers to be more prevalent among Union forces. Charles Walcott, of the Twenty-first Massachusetts Volunteers, attributed the Federal plundering around Frederick to camp followers and stragglers. This same disregard of citizen property and military orders continued on the march westward through the Middletown area. He remarked that the half-starved Rebel army did not even pick ripe apples from the trees. In contrast, the well-provided-for Union troops consumed an abundance of fruit, chickens and young pigs on their march to Sharpsburg.[56] For Lewis H. Steiner, inspector for the Sanitary Commission in Frederick at the time, the greater obedience and discipline of the Confederate forces in 1862 was partially attributable to General Lee's stringent orders to respect citizen property in Maryland. But he also observed, "When separated from their officers, they do not show the same self-reliance that our men possess."[57] It should be noted that while the restraints mandated by Lee in 1862 probably reduced some of the pillaging by his army, the changing dynamics of the war and the desperation of the Confederates led them in 1864 to despoil the Maryland countryside. Revenge against what were considered the "enemy's atrocities" contributed to Union major general David Hunter's campaign of destruction in the Virginia's Shenandoah Valley, followed by their opponent's burning of the town of Chambersburg. The standards of behavior toward civilians and their property were lowered for both sides as the war continued into its third year.

Historians have examined in great detail the discipline issues in the Civil War. Lorien Foote, in the book *The Gentlemen and the Roughs: Violence,*

Soldiers stealing a bull from villagers. *Library of Congress.*

Honor and Manhood in the Union Army, identified part of the problem as the competing conceptions of manhood that were played out against the backdrop of camp. Army regulations stressed moral rectitude, restrained behavior and avoidance of drinking, fighting, gambling and profanity. Chaplains and the United States Christian Commission supported the army hierarchy in promoting these behavioral expectations. However, the "roughs," as Foote called them, lived by a different code of conduct that was based on a "culture of male camaraderie centered on boisterous noise, unruly behavior, and feats of prowess." These were the men who got drunk, called out their officers and fought with one another and occasionally with the civilians they encountered while outside of camp. Other men who were not the "roughs" also were willing at times to fight when their honor was challenged because this mark of character had to be validated by peers for their own sense of self-worth. Foote argued that class tensions within the army increased as substitutes, immigrants and conscripts swelled the ranks, leading to a further crackdown by officers on misconduct.[58]

Historian Steven J. Ramold, in 2010, completed an exhaustive and comprehensive study of discipline in the Union army in his treatise *Baring the Iron Hand*. Ramold was careful to distinguish between two types of discipline—that associated with camp and that of the battlefield. He argued that the latter was the "traditional measurement of combat efficiency: the willingness to enter battle, risk one's life and kill the enemy." Although it took some time to organize, drill and train the forces properly, the ultimate success of the Union in the war testified to its combat effectiveness. Such was not the case with discipline in and outside of camp. Here, according to Ramold, the course of the war was characterized by a clash between the military hierarchy's desire to maintain regulations and the strictures of middle-class Victorian morality versus the unwillingness of many soldiers to follow any code. Instead, they "created their own definition of morality in a military environment of long boredom, hard living, and early death." What the author called "fringe behaviors"—those that were frowned on but not explicitly banned by the Articles of War—often escalated into much more serious trouble as soldiers tested the limits of what their officers would tolerate.[59]

Soldiers perceived their weapons as "extensions of themselves" and "seemed to squeeze off shots whenever, and at whatever, the fancy struck them, despite the efforts of officers to control them." Ramold and many other historians emphasized that the alcohol problem in the ranks was of epic proportions and was a major contributing factor to the defiance of regulations and the outbreaks of violence both within camp and out in the streets. As the war progressed and soldiers were exposed to horrific sights on the battlefield, the level of property and violent crimes escalated. Some soldiers now committed acts that in their antebellum days would have "stained a man's reputation, created public outcry, and led to lengthy prison terms, or even the death penalty. In the chaos of war, traditional modes of behavior changed, and actions that would have stunned them in civilian life, became acceptable or even expected." The result of all of this, according to Ramold, was at least eighty thousand general courts-martial. Since most infractions of military regulations were handled in regimental courts-martial, the total number of legal proceedings was impossible to estimate.[60] While this was but a small fraction of the over two million soldiers serving in the Union army during the war, it represented a significant problem for military authorities.

While Ramold and Foote were concerned with more serious transgressions of military discipline and even criminal law, historian Bell Irvin Wiley discovered that lesser, but more commonplace, vices increased during the war. In his seminal work, *The Life of Billy Yank: The Common Soldier of the Union,* he discussed the eternal struggle between good and evil in and out of camp and concluded that there were very real problems with behaviors such as profanity, gambling, drinking, prostitution and use of pornography among the troops on both sides in the Civil War. Wiley attributed the degeneration in morals to "the removal of accustomed restraints and associations, the urge to experiment with the forbidden, the desire to escape boredom and the utter inadequacy of religious and recreational facilities for soldiers."[61] While military authorities and chaplains attempted to discourage such activities, with the exception of excessive drinking, these behaviors cited by Wiley were far less likely to impact the civilian population.

In the military, the provost marshal's office was in charge of maintaining order and discipline within the ranks, and provost guards were the ones responsible for finding and arresting those involved in deserting, straggling, drinking, leaving camp without a pass and other violations of military codes. The authorities were told to follow the Articles of War adopted by Congress in 1806 that established military policies relating to discipline and conduct. Section 32 specified that if officers or soldiers were found "beating or otherwise ill-treating any person, or disturbing fairs or markets, or of committing any kind of riots, to the disquieting of the citizens of the United States," the commander was to take punitive action to ensure justice. Section 33 concerned any capital crime, use of violence or offense against a citizen's person or property and provided for action against the soldier or officer responsible.[62] These Articles of War were supplemented by the Lieber Code, promulgated by President

Three Union soldiers. *Library of Congress.*

Lincoln as General Orders No. 100 in April 1863 and designed to provide some protections for civilians in occupied areas. Particularly significant was Article 37: "The United States acknowledge and protect, in hostile countries occupied by them, religion and morality; strictly private property; the persons of the inhabitants, especially those of women; and the sacredness of domestic relations. Offenses to the contrary shall be rigorously punished." This same code outlawed rape, theft, pillaging, and vandalism but authorized the confiscation of private property if the officer in charge approved and intended to use the materials for military purposes.[63]

In Maryland, the department commanders issued orders for the men to follow when outside of camp. They were very similar regardless of location within the state and included the following: soldiers were not permitted to go into the city without a pass issued by an officer or the provost marshal; those with passes were to return by 7:30 (or 8:00) p.m. if not on duty; they were not to take their arms; and their horses were to trot, not gallop, through

Staff of the Office of Provost Marshal in Cumberland. *Library of Congress.*

the streets. Merchants and tavern owners were not permitted to sell or serve alcohol to men in uniform. General N. Banks offered some additional advice: "All commanders ought to encourage useful occupations and manly exercises and diversions among their men, and to repress dissipation and immorality."[64] This guidance must have seemed naïve to many of those who left their camps, with or without passes, and sought the creature comforts offered by brothels, merchants, taverns, groggeries and restaurants in nearby towns and cities.

While the military regulations and orders for soldiers to obey were generally clear and consistent in all sites within the military department, the implementation at the unit level varied widely. The large number of violations, arrests and incarcerations of soldiers in Baltimore indicated a lack of effective oversight and enforcement by officers in many cases. However, there were exceptions. George Perkins of the 149th Ohio Volunteer Infantry was on picket duty for a time at Fort No. Eleven in the city when twelve cavalrymen arrived in full gallop. Then the commanding officer ordered them to fire at two deserters who were running through the field. In an instant, both were dead. Perkins described the discipline in his unit as "severe," but he believed that it was necessary because of the "great variety of characters that made up the army." The persistent troublemakers he singled out were the rough men from the New York Artillery who delighted in bullying the new soldiers who had just arrived. When two inmates from the New York unit escaped from the guardhouse, Perkins and others shot at them. The attempted jailbreak was foiled, but the clearly frightened men, who were found and then captured in a ditch, confessed that they did not believe the "century plants" (Hundred Days men) would shoot at them.[65]

At the other end of the discipline spectrum in Baltimore was the camp of the Baltimore Battery of Light Artillery located on the outskirts of the city near the Jones Falls. There, according to their biographer Frederick Wild, the supervision was exceedingly lenient. He noted, "Our officers were very liberal with passes to leave camp, nor were there any severe punishments inflicted upon those who were caught leaving camp without a pass." The result was that over half of the men on any given night left camp after 8:00 p.m. roll call, went to the city and did not return until roll call the following morning. Undoubtedly, some of these men were visiting family or friends. Wild found much the same lax environment when he was at Camp Parole in Annapolis as a paroled POW returned from Belle Isle. He said that he heard that the officers did not care how many were AWOL because they "kept drawing money for the full amount of prisoners whether they were in camp or not." As a result, he and others donned civilian clothes and headed for Baltimore without any passes.[66]

Alfred Davenport, a Duryee Zouave stationed at Fort Federal Hill, located on Baltimore's harbor, explained that enforcement of regulations on leave became a contest for supremacy between the officers and the enlistees. The latter enjoyed the risk and excitement of outwitting the authorities, and in turn, officers and guards had to exercise all the ingenuity they possessed to deal with potential escapees, resorting to such tactics as disguising themselves as privates or hiding in the bushes and spying on the troublemakers. Davenport observed that thirty or forty soldiers would elude the one hundred guards on duty and depart from the fort every night, not to return until before reveille the next morning. On Federal Hill, a man they called "Jack Sheppard" managed to escape camp with two pairs of handcuffs on his wrists linked to a ball and chain on his foot. Another habitual offender of regulations explained that he joined the army to fight the enemy, not to be cooped up in an enclosure. Identifying and catching those who went AWOL were all the more problematic because men rarely, if ever, betrayed a comrade to the authorities: "A regiment is like a large family—their interests are the same; they rely each one on the honor of the other for effectiveness and protection."[67]

Being absent without leave from camp was one of the most frequently reported violations of regulations, and it was certainly the source of many problems between soldiers and civilians. Exceeding curfew and simply failing to show up at morning roll call were commonplace offenses. During the month of August in 1861, police in Baltimore arrested 171 soldiers and sent them to their camps for review and punishment. Major General Wool, head of the Middle Department, issued General Order No. 61 on December 9, 1862, requiring the arrests of all men without passes, resulting in the apprehension of 134 soldiers in just one night of that week. The *Sun* newspaper on January 31, 1864, complained about the military's failure to enforce the curfew, noting that 38 men representing ten to twelve different commands were picked up and taken to the central police station the night before.[68] Not surprisingly, the records of the Baltimore Light Artillery indicated that the most frequent charge against its men was being absent without leave, represented in the roster books as failure to show up for roll call at five o'clock in the morning.[69] These issues were present throughout the state. As reported by the *Valley Register* of Middletown, orders were promulgated that any soldiers absent without leave would be hunted down; the paper added that the military was occupying a loyal population, and they "look to [soldiers] for the preservation of order and discipline."[70]

Soldiers willing to risk jail time or other punishment for failure to have a pass were often the same individuals who were frequenting the houses of ill fame (as they were called back then) or patronizing the bars. Lacking supervision and often drinking heavily, these men got in fights with one another and with civilians. Some of them bore responsibility for vandalism, arson and other property crimes and for a surprising number of attacks involving guns, knives, clubs and even swords. They found safety and psychological support in numbers and often committed crimes in the presence, or with the help, of other soldiers. They fought over politics, women, threats to their honor, anger over an officer's orders or just plain boredom.

The reasons for the disciplinary problems in the Federal army were complex, multifaceted and evolving as the war continued. The Union's use of the draft, the employment of substitutes and the enticement of bounties to enlist all had the effect of incorporating into the military men whose motivation and morale were at times questionable. Martin Haynes, of the Second New Hampshire, stationed as a guard at Point Lookout Prison in the fall of 1863, complained bitterly about the substitutes and the trouble that they caused his unit. Extra guards were required, and the boats were taken away in order to prevent these men from escaping. Haynes said of this in his journal, "So much extra work for the boys, all on account of these human vermin New Hampshire is filling up her old units with."[71] Frequently, the men who enlisted complained about the lack of discipline of the "new soldier," who appeared for the wrong reasons and was more likely to be found in the ranks of the bounty-jumpers, deserters, slackers or stragglers. Men who fell into one of these categories tended to cause the most trouble for their comrades, the authorities and civilians.

Violence was less shocking and appalling to men who had been in battle and had witnessed at close range the grisly and gruesome mangling and deaths of their comrades. Warren Freeman, of the Thirteenth Massachusetts, writing to his father shortly after the Battle of Antietam, spoke for many when he acknowledged the impact of battle on soldiers: "The scenes of blood and strife," he wrote, "that I have been called to pass through during the months that are passed, and my 'baptism in blood,' have nearly destroyed all the finer feelings of my nature."[72] Captain Robert G. Carter explained his frame of mind at Sharpsburg in 1862:

> *You have no idea what a life this is; none but the strongest, the iron constitution, can stand it. It is the roughest, toughest life I have ever experienced…The sights I have seen, death in every form; the cutting of limbs, the suffering I have endured, beside seeing others suffer, the discouragement I have met with, have taken the spirit out of me.*[73]

Many of these men were still in their late teens and early twenties (the average age of the Civil War soldier was 25.8 years), so their youth and inexperience with the vicissitudes of life made it more difficult to adapt to the horrors of battle and to the rigorous demands of the military.

Execution by firing squad of five deserters. *Library of Congress.*

The impact of exposure to combat on the human mind was acknowledged in the Civil War but poorly understood. There were occasional references in diaries, journals and letters to "derangement of mind," "depression" and "mania" in an attempt to explain mood and behavior. Research in the last decade involving soldiers from coalition nations returning home from Iraq and Afghanistan indicated that men and women in those combat zones were subjected to a distinctive set of stressors that affected both physical and mental health. An analysis from the Institute of Medicine in 2013 showed that returning service members from the above wars had rates "as high as 20 percent for PSTD, 37 percent for depression and 39 percent for alcohol abuse."[74] Similar conclusions were reached in the same year by Australian researchers who found a fifteen-fold increase in mental health problems of their soldiers stationed for lengthy periods in the Middle East Area of Operations.[75] Extended or multiple deployments, exposure to shot and shell, the death of comrades, the burying process and the ever-present fear of one's own death all took a toll on the well-being and mental stability of soldiers and auxiliary personnel. These same general conditions were present for soldiers in the Civil War. Any attempt to understand the problems with discipline and the soldiers' relationship with civilians must start with a recognition that the traumatic effects of combat extended beyond the battlefield and beyond the termination of service.

3

Soldiers versus Civilians

There is always a lot of skulkers and robbers in the rear of the army who never intended to do anything but rob, and who never get into battle.[76]
—*W.A. Roberts, Forty-fifth Pennsylvania Infantry*

In March 1865, the staunchly unionist *Frederick Examiner* urged Provost Marshal Major Braugher to institute stricter measures whereby the "frequent repetition of acts of rowdyism witnessed in streets may be effectively restrained. A painful degree of insecurity is felt by our citizens, many of whom keep within doors at night through fear of being insulted and knocked down by drunken and disorderly soldiers." Residents of Frederick and other cities in Maryland were justified in their apprehension. When the *Baltimore Sun* printed the city crime report for August 1863, it noted that the number of soldiers or deserters temporarily lodged in jails exceeded that of civilians arrested for offenses against the law. This was true also in the September crime report for that year.[77] Soldiers were arrested in notable numbers for desertion, straggling, breaking curfew, property crimes and serious crimes. This inevitably had a negative impact on the civilian population because it challenged the conventional belief, at least among the unionists, that they were there to defend the residents and to maintain order and safety.

The errant soldiers who repeatedly got in trouble were but a small minority of the Union forces, but their impact was larger than their numbers. These were the rogues and misfits of the army who believed that

Camp of Massachusetts Second Company, Light Artillery, in Baltimore. *Library of Congress.*

drinking, plundering, fistfighting and insubordination were the hallmarks of the manly soldier. These troublemakers were more likely to be found among the stragglers, deserters, teamsters and substitutes, according to the comments made by other Union soldiers not in those categories. Charles Francis Adams Jr., of the Fifth Massachusetts Cavalry, disturbed by the pillaging by Union soldiers in the Antietam campaign, had a suggestion: "By establishing guards and making straggling the highest military offense, you could not only divest war of its main horrors, as far as non-combatants are concerned, but you could stop the greatest cause of demoralization."[78]

The issue of incentives was a critical one. Men had many reasons not to volunteer to serve, including fear, family responsibilities, health issues, pacifism or lack of support for the war or the Lincoln administration. Those who were compelled by the draft or enticed only by bounties or substitute fees were generally less motivated and less likely to be amenable to the discipline required by their officers. Some draftees went to extraordinary lengths, including suicide and self-mutilation, to avoid or end their service. A Pennsylvania man slit his own throat in the Union Relief Association Rooms in Baltimore because he did not want to be in the military; however, he survived. At Camp Carroll a soldier tried to commit suicide by stabbing himself no fewer than a dozen times, and in 1864 an unknown soldier hanged himself on the Almshouse Farm near the Baltimore City limits.[79] Chaplain Richard Eddy, of the Sixtieth New York, discussed a sudden monomania of behavior as six or eight men in his regiment shot off their thumb or fingers. In each of these cases, was it an accident or an attempt to earn a discharge?[80]

Some of the behavior of the soldiers in Maryland seemed inexplicable at the time, and perhaps it was due to mental illness, post-traumatic stress disorder, gang mentality or simply gross immaturity. Baltimore City residents visiting Lexington Market must have shaken their heads in befuddlement when a soldier from the Third Maryland Cavalry came into the facility and started to break the dishes of the women who engaged in selling pottery. When a bystander tried to stop this destruction, he was stabbed for his intervention. Even more bizarre were the actions of six soldiers from the Ninety-first New York Regiment, who were arrested for throwing vitriol on ladies' dresses and cloaks as they came out of several churches on Eastern Avenue and Charles Street in the city. In an incident that the *Baltimore Clipper* called a "terrible affair," a train with six hundred soldiers on board stopped for a while in Beltsville, and "the soldiers on it amused themselves by throwing apples at the Veteran Reserve Corps and calling them epithets," questioning their honor and their courage. As a result, Sergeant Porter of the Veteran Reserve Guard picked up a musket and fired on the train, killing one and injuring another. Soldiers from the train then got out, beat Porter mercilessly and bayonetted him to death.[81]

While many of the crimes committed by soldiers were attacks on their comrades or their officers, quite a number of the occurrences involved civilians who were far less likely to possess weapons to defend themselves. Incidents started early in the war and continued until the military withdrew from the state in 1866. In August 1861, several soldiers from the forces of Major General Banks ransacked and then burned a few homes, arguing in their defense that they were houses of prostitution. Around the same time, two soldiers from a Pennsylvania regiment broke into a law office in Monrovia to steal money. As the war was ending in April 1865, soldiers robbed a jewelry store in Frederick of watches and rings, and in the following month in that city, a group of Federals brutally attacked a young man and fractured his skull. This last episode led the local newspaper editors to express once again their frustration with the military's failure to ameliorate the violence. They noted, "We had hoped that when the war terminated that the scenes of rowdyism so frequently enacted on our streets would also terminate and good order be maintained, but in this we have been disappointed."[82] Meanwhile, in Annapolis in May 1865, two soldiers were arrested on the suspicion that they were responsible for a wave of arsons plaguing the state's capital.[83]

George Frederick Elliott, of the First Connecticut Artillery, in a letter to his father written soon after Union troops occupied Hagerstown, mentioned that he was about a mile and a half out of town doing guard duty. One object, according to him, was "to protect the citizens of the town from the abuse which they…would receive from a certain class of soldiers who [may] have obtained a pass or have escaped the camp by running the Guard stationed around it."[84] At Liverpool Point on the Potomac in southern Maryland, the Thirteenth New Hampshire Volunteer Infantry posted a guard over the house of Mr. Childs when members of a New Jersey regiment posed a threat to his family. The soldiers were trying to burglarize his house, so his eighteen-year-old daughter brazenly pulled out a gun and shot at the men. They then got in a scuffle with her, and in the process, most of her clothes were torn off. She fled, and the men were unable to catch her, but it was clear that these individuals were trouble. The New Jersey men, very soon after the previous incident, also stole pigs from a local farm even though a guard had been posted at that location.[85]

Military authorities were justifiably concerned with depredations on the private property of residents in their districts. Stephen H. Bogardus, who was a member of the Purnell Legion stationed at Chapel Point in Maryland, revealed in his diary on January 24, 1864, that squads of cavalry within his unit were causing trouble for local residents by pillaging and destroying public and private property in the area, even though they were in the presence of commissioned officers.[86] Captain Janvrin W. Graves, of the Fifth Regiment New Hampshire Volunteers, disclosed that when his unit camped on the way from Rockville to Sharpsburg, Colonel Cross, his commanding officer, ran a sword through a farmer's pig. They also killed a calf, resulting in a delicious breakfast of leg of fresh pig and a kettle of veal stew. When the owner of the livestock came down to camp and demanded an explanation, Cross denied any wrongdoing on the part of his men.[87] Lieutenant E.L. Cowart, of the Fourteenth New Jersey, in a letter to his cousin about a month after the Battle of Monocacy, bemoaned the consequences of the lax attitude toward citizens' property: "Oh, what a curse is resting on the chief operators of this doleful struggle: it would make your heart ache to see the view of property; the tears of the destitute, cries of woman or child, or take the only cow from which the little baby derive their daily nourishment."[88]

In major campaigns, such as those resulting in the Battles of Antietam and Gettysburg, the sheer number of soldiers streaming through a region was enough to do major damage in agricultural communities and villages. As the 118th Pennsylvania Volunteers marched through Maryland, "it was quite apparent the only purpose of the pursuers and pursued was to get along as rapidly as possible, regardless of what was lost, mutilated, or forgotten." When the soldiers reached Middletown, they found that the residents had removed all handles from the pumps because they believed that overuse would exhaust their water supply. When some of the thirsty men sought a drink and were blocked, they took out their anger by throwing objects such as stones and trash down the wells in the town.[89] According to Richard Tylden Auchmuty, of the Fifth Army Corps, the traffic in soldiers returning from Gettysburg was so large in the Hagerstown area that for miles the farmers' crops were trampled to death at the height of the growing season: "The Marylanders seem stunned by the destruction of their property, and came in crowds to know what to do." Auchmuty observed that since they were loyal, they would receive politeness from the army, but not much else.[90]

Plundering citizens' property had serious unintended consequences at times. An incident, related by Francis H. Buffum of the Fourteenth New Hampshire Regiment, concerned the common practice of visiting nearby farms and stealing straw. One of the soldiers on such a mission came back to camp with a bullet hole in his hand and another in his leg. In a short time,

Miller House at Antietam. Residents living on or near battlefields were in danger. *Library of Congress.*

the men got together, their excitement and anger escalated and they plotted revenge against the shooter, including the possibility of raiding Poolesville, the nearby town, and burning down the entire farm of the civilian who fired the weapon. Their colonel discovered their plans, doubled the guards and ordered the shooting of any man who attempted to leave camp that night. Buffum noted that if the colonel had not taken such stringent action, the men involved would have forever sullied the reputation of their regiment by carrying out the planned action. "It showed," he said, "that, under certain conditions, a military camp is a very inflammable and dangerous establishment."[91]

At those times when the military personnel legitimately confiscated private property for military uses, they were supposed to leave receipts for the owners that would allow them to receive remuneration for their losses. This was precisely what happened when the First Delaware Cavalry came though the Unionville area of Frederick County during the Confederates'

1864 invasion. Twenty-five residents got notices from Captain Caleb Churchman that they would receive payment for the cows, goats, horses, etc., that the Union took from them. James Pearre, one of those victimized farmers, complained that he never received his money until he secured the influence of John W. Garrett, president of the B&O Railroad.[92] The line between legitimate use of private property for military purposes and outright pillaging was frequently crossed, and officers seldom punished those involved, particularly in the last two years of the war. Confederate sympathizers were most easily victimized, rarely compensated for property loss and sometimes deliberately targeted.

Union soldiers bent on mischief were able to intimidate some Maryland residents. The *Sun* reported that soldiers from the Patterson Park camp in Baltimore were visiting dry goods and variety stores on Eastern Avenue and requesting that the merchants provide them with certain items without payment. Three soldiers went into a place of business on Lombard Street and demanded merchandise from an elderly lady. When she told them that she was very poor, they took the items anyway. The *Sun* complained that this kind of theft was happening every night in the city.[93] Those in the military guarding the state's railroads at times also took advantage of their position to terrorize civilians. Major General Wool notified Halleck that one of the soldiers of the 118th New York Volunteers at the Relay House had killed an engineer of the Washington train, and the culprit was now in jail. He mentioned, "Threats were made that other injuries might be done to passing trains…I therefore deemed it best to send the regiment where it would do no harm."[94] The secessionist newspaper the *South* reported on another nearly tragic episode that occurred on one of the B&O trains arriving into Baltimore with excess speed. As it came into the station, the picket guard fired repeatedly at the railcars. The train was riddled with bullets, as startled women and children passengers sought the safety of the floor that was covered with splintered glass.[95] This type of dangerous and inappropriate firing of weapons in public places justifiably alarmed civilians.

Trains were often the venues of clashes between soldiers and civilians. In July 1861, several soldiers were smoking on the railway, in violation of the rules. When the conductor tried to eject them, he was attacked with a knife. In the same month, there was a confrontation between a secessionist supporter and a Union soldier over the war, and when a fistfight broke out, the conductor threw both of them off the train. Another episode that captured the public's attention involved a soldier who attempted to force kisses on a female passenger. When the startled woman shrieked, the conductor stopped

Ruins of the B&O Railroad Bridge over the Potomac at Harpers Ferry. *Library of Congress.*

the train and dealt a blow to the head of the offender. This event led the *Baltimore Sun* to editorialize on the danger of further trouble. Noting that several regiments contained Hundred Days men whose service was about to expire, the newspaper warned that conflicts could increase because any offenders heading home "will escape detection and accountability." They urged people "to be on guard under any necessary exposure to indignity or assault, as our citizens have been rendered almost helpless for their own defense and protection."[96]

Violence associated with ideological differences was also apparent in Maryland during the war. Soldiers of the Fourth Regiment Potomac Home Brigade destroyed and gutted a lager beer saloon in Frederick in 1862 because some of the patrons inside were drinking a toast to Jefferson Davis. Diarist Jacob Engelbrecht said that it was done in a very methodical manner, as the vandals posted guards outside to prevent any interruption of their work.[97] Walter Dunn, a Union soldier stationed in Baltimore, wrote to a friend about an incident that he witnessed on the streets in July 1863. As

Kate Chase Sprague with Union officers. *Library of Congress.*

Confederate POWs were marching through the city, a citizen called for three cheers for Jefferson Davis. Surprisingly, the surgeon in charge of Jarvis Hospital knocked the offending man down, and then a Union cavalryman ran up and started attacking the Southern sympathizer's head with his saber. Dunn said the cavalryman "would have killed him" had not some bystander dragged him out of the fracas.[98] Divergent views of the war, whether real or perceived, were responsible for a similar incident early in the war. Two *Baltimore Sun* employees were visiting a camp near Federal Hill and got into a discussion with the soldiers about the guns trained on the city. A soldier accused one of the reporters of being a secessionist and started to beat, kick and knock him to the ground with other soldiers joining in the affray. Fortunately, the police and some of the other men from the fort came to the injured man's assistance. Symbols such as flags often provoked unpleasant or even violent confrontations between citizens and soldiers. At a meeting of peace advocates, men from the New York Scott Life Guards stationed in Port Deposit intervened and demanded that an American flag be raised at the site. A bloody riot ensued in which two citizens were stabbed to death, and one or two of the soldiers were wounded. Seven of the soldiers were indicted for killing the civilians; however, all but one of them escaped the guardhouse, resulting in an immediate search.[99]

Civilians in Baltimore witnessed a number of riots and affrays, including a major breach of peace involving the Twenty-third Pennsylvania Regiment that was at the Union Relief Rooms in August 1864. Some of them left, found whiskey and then went to a lager beer saloon. They got very intoxicated, and then two of their members beat up a sergeant. When the provost guard arrived to arrest the Pennsylvania soldiers, other members of their regiment rushed in with arms to aid their comrades. A massive riot occurred that spilled out into the street, where bricks were thrown, pistols were discharged and dozens were injured as men, women and children watched in shock and horror. The rioters returned to the Union Relief Rooms, smashing and damaging furniture and objects until Provost Marshal Colonel Woolley made an appearance with pistol and sword drawn. When armed help came to the scene from all over the city, Woolley was finally able to calm everyone down. The Pennsylvania troops involved departed Baltimore on the train late that night. It was noted in the newspaper that the men in question were Philadelphia firefighters, who went off to war with 1,500 men and now numbered only 250.[100] The psychological impact of losing that proportion of one's unit to the ravages of disease and to the slaughterhouse of the battlefield was unimaginable. Under the circumstances, it was easier to understand why they would hurry to the defense of their comrades when they believed a threat existed, even if it was one ignited by their own misbehavior.

Undisciplined soldiers acted at times as if they did not care whom they victimized. Early in the war, a soldier named Patrick Barker deliberately tripped an elderly man on Federal Hill, resulting in a broken leg.[101] Two soldiers of the Second Maryland were walking in the streets when one of them stabbed an aged black man with his bayonet, inflicting possibly a fatal wound. In this case and in a number of others, it was not known if the episode was racially motivated. The old gentleman was scolding some boys for throwing bricks in his yard when the attack occurred. In another incident, a boy selling lemonade in the streets near the Soldiers' Rest got into a dispute with a member of the First Delaware Regiment over the price of the drink, when suddenly the angry soldier shot the boy. A broad search was necessary in order to hunt down and arrest the alleged offender. In a similarly inexplicable event, three young children lost their twenty-nine-year-old father when he was mortally wounded by a member of the Purnell Legion Cavalry. When the two men accidently collided in the street, the irate soldier shot the civilian. Another murder occurred in a dispute over property in Point of Rocks. Mr. Calvin Lamar, who was visiting that location on his handcar, got into a quarrel with some soldiers who wanted to borrow it. They followed him home, words were again exchanged and Samuel Webster of a New Hampshire regiment shot Lamar in the head. He died instantly.[102]

Rape by soldiers was a crime of concern to women and their loved ones who lived in occupied areas. Historian Stephen V. Ash maintained that this was a relatively rare occurrence, but it did occur, particularly in isolated areas and by unsupervised men like deserters and stragglers. More common, according to Ash, was "symbolic rape," which involved invading and violating a woman's privacy and sense of security, using obscene language, exposure of private parts and other indecencies.[103] Crystal N. Feimster, author of *Southern Horrors: Women and the Politics of Rape and Lynching*, noted, "Union military courts prosecuted at least 450 cases involving sexual crimes."[104] Given the reluctance of the victims to speak about or report rape, it was obviously more prevalent than the figures indicated. A particularly brutal case involved eight soldiers from the camp of the Fourth New York Volunteers near Rock River Bridge at North Point and Philadelphia Roads. A woman was raped, and her male companion, who was with her at the time, was so badly injured by the New York soldiers that he was not expected to survive. The young man eventually recovered and testified about the crime: "He does not doubt

Burning of Chambersburg. *Library of Congress.*

that they intended to kill him. The young lady was not yet in a state to be removed home. When news of the outrage transpired, the most intense excitement was created in the neighborhood, and organizations for a search were immediately made." A Hagerstown newspaper reported that Joseph Glazier, a soldier with the Thirteenth Massachusetts Regiment, was arrested by the sheriff for the attempted rape of "a very highly respectable lady, wife of Mr. Michael Funk."[105] The discipline problems recounted here were not unique to the Union army, a fact that was readily apparent to Marylanders, many of whom witnessed both sides in action.

Citizen soldiers, who constituted the vast majority in Civil War armies, represented a broad cross-section of American society and contained within their ranks individuals of both dubious and high moral character. At times during their service, they were confronted with ethical quandaries that challenged the sensibilities of most soldiers. They were empowered with the ability to damage property, to harm humans and to make life and death decisions on the battlefield. Some soldiers took this responsibility very seriously, while others went about their work thoughtlessly, as was apparent in the burning of the town of Chambersburg, just north of the Mason-Dixon line. Confederate Maryland and Virginia cavalry brigades, under the joint command of Brigadier Generals Bradley T. Johnson and John McCausland, were ordered to ransom the town and, if the money was not forthcoming, to burn it. Colonel William Peters was given instructions to start the fire, but he asked to be relieved of this burden. According to Captain George W. Booth, Major Harry Gilmor did the deed instead with "promptness and zeal." Booth's explanation for Gilmor's actions was simple: "He was not troubled with compunctions which affected Colonel Peters; in fact, he was a different type of mental and moral manhood." When McCausland later threatened to burn the town of Hancock, Maryland, unless officials there paid a ransom, Brigadier General Johnson objected, and another discussion ensued, cut short by the arrival of the Federals.[106] Since actions such as these were intentional direct threats to civilians, some of the soldiers were deeply troubled by what they considered to be ethically objectionable tactics, but others had no such reservations.

Both sides committed what some saw as atrocities, others as justifiable revenge for the enemy's actions and still others as the brutal but essential means of subduing the opponent and ending the war more quickly. On the macro level, both Union and Confederate armies escalated the hard war approach as the conflict dragged on and the death toll climbed. They sought to wage a war of terror, hoping to break the will and morale of the enemy and the supporting civilian population. On the micro level, each individual soldier had to make difficult choices of conscience routinely as part of his mission. A small minority of the men were simply rogues—misbehaving soldiers who were not troubled by drinking, looting, burning, assaulting one another and civilians or undermining their cause by their own misconduct. Both officers and enlisted men knew that these disciplinary problems were facilitated by alcohol misuse.

4

John Barleycorn and the Enablers

Whiskey rules this army. I don't like whiskey for a commander. If I should tell you one half of what I know you would not wonder that the soldiers have lost their patriotism.[107]
—*Herbert George, July 24, 1864*

R obert C. Schenck issued an important General Order in Baltimore in March 1863. In it, he stated, "It has been brought to the attention of the Major General Commanding that much of the disorder and misconduct of the soldiers of this command has been occasioned by the habit of frequenting or visiting places where spirituous liquors are sold to them by inconsiderate or unprincipled persons." Schenck then ordered the arrest of any soldier found in such a place and mandated that those who sold to his men would have their bars shut down.[108] All of the military commanders who claimed part of Maryland as their jurisdiction made similar observations and decrees regarding the punishments imposed on those involved. These attempts were often in vain. Alcohol abuse remained a serious problem among both enlistees and officers who were seeking solace, oblivion, joy, forgetfulness or comfort in the bottle and saw little reason to forego one of the few pleasures offered by military life in the Civil War. Drinking whiskey was a mark of masculinity to some, facilitating socializing and relieving the boredom of camp. Unfortunately, it led at times to dereliction of duty, accidents, fistfights and crime. It was a contributory factor in 18 percent of the cases that came before general courts-martial and for many more of those brought to regimental courts-martial and to field officer courts.[109]

Civil War soldiers, regardless of where they were located, were ingenious in their methods for finding liquor. On Maryland Heights at Harpers Ferry, men of the Baltimore Battery of Light Artillery found a "whiskey station" in a temporary shed under a ledge on the very steep mountain.[110] Alcohol was smuggled into camp in canteens, on the bottom of barrels or boxes, in fake coconut shells, in belts and in large pockets of coats.[111] It was sent in packages from friends and relatives. Henry Ropes, of the Twentieth Massachusetts Regiment, wrote a simple request to his brother: "Send me a flask that doesn't leak and fill it with the *very best* brandy."[112] When soldiers were stationed at a single site for an extended period of time, men were known to brew their own beer or alcoholic beverages with slang names like "Bust Head" and "Oh Be Joyful." Teamsters, stragglers and deserters, considered the dregs of the army and often found beyond the oversight of officers, excelled in the hunt and discovery of new sources of the much sought-after liquor. Sutlers were major vendors of alcohol, although they risked expulsion from camp if they were caught. In addition, despite the prohibitions against selling alcohol to soldiers, there were always merchants and tavern owners whose love of money exceeded their fear of the provost marshal.

Second Lieutenant Stephen M. Weld from Camp Holmes, near Annapolis, wrote to his father that forty gallons of liquor were found at military headquarters, evidently brought into camp by soldiers' friends. Weld noted that when they were on the train, at every station they stopped, they had to prevent civilians selling alcohol from reaching the soldiers on board. He mentioned that they had to shoot at one man because he would not get away from the cars. In a subsequent letter home, he said that some soldiers were so drunk and disorderly when they came back into camp that they had to tie them up to restore quiet. One particularly egregious and repeat offender, a man named Casey, was tied up by the thumbs and gagged. After he kicked one officer, was warned and then kicked another, Weld shot Casey twice, once in the arm and once in the mouth. The bayonet used to gag him saved his life.[113] Drunk officers and men bedeviled Brigadier General Willoughby, who was at that time stationed at Fort McHenry. On July 29, 1861, he stated that fewer than two hundred men were left in camp that evening, and four or five officers were under arrest: "A hundred men are drunk, a hundred more are at houses of ill-fame, and the balance are everywhere...Colonel Alford is very drunk all of the time now. We shall not endure him much longer."[114]

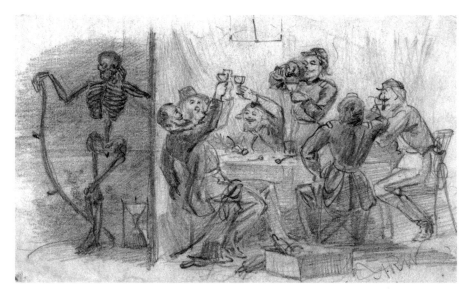

Soldiers' Toast: "Here's to health of the next one that dies." *Library of Congress.*

Soldiers drinking and playing cards in front of the flag. *Library of Congress.*

At times, the drinking was so widespread that it was virtually impossible to single out those responsible for initiating the problem, particularly if civilians were involved. Women selling whiskey in canteens approached troops who were waiting in line for a train to Frederick in July 1863. The thirsty men from the 144th New York Regiment, who were in transit to assist General Meade's pursuit of General Robert E. Lee's retreating army, decided to imbibe. By the time the train was on its way, "in most cars pandemonium reigned until the excesses of the drinking men ended in sleep or drunken stupor." The soldiers, gleeful and filled with a spirit of generosity, shared their whiskey with the train crew, who also became inebriated. As a result, when the train stopped at Monocacy Junction just south of Frederick, the crew failed to flag the next train, which was carrying troops from the 142nd New York and the 40th Massachusetts. The second train then rammed the first, resulting in sixteen soldiers being sent to the hospital, a major blockage on the tracks and a delay of the reinforcements for Meade's army by one day. One of the soldiers who witnessed this debacle later wondered if four thousand fresh men might have made a difference in intercepting some of the Confederates involved in Lee's retreat from Gettysburg back to Virginia.[115]

For many of the soldiers who would end up in Gettysburg, the march to get there was unrelenting and grueling. As they passed through Maryland, someone in the 141st Pennsylvania Regiment suggested that the walking would be easier if they had some liquor. Through some means, a "considerable number of the boys in the corps procured whiskey, and instead of it being a help on the march it proved to be a hindrance, for they grew very tired before they had gone a half-dozen miles. Some of them were too drunk, and had to be left behind."[116] In Manchester, just a few miles from Gettysburg, intoxicated men were thrown in the bushes for cavalry squads or provost guards to pick up later, or they faced the possibility of capture by the Confederates.[117]

Stragglers and deserters were frequently the worst offenders of regulations on alcohol. This was the case in Frederick as the Union army made its way north to meet Lee's army in Gettysburg in 1863. Whitelaw Reid, observing the scene, wrote graphically of what happened there for the *Cincinnati Gazette*:

> *Frederick is Pandemonium. Somebody has blundered frightfully: the town is filled with stragglers, and the liquor shops are in full blast. Just under my windows scores of drunken soldiers are making the night hideous: all over town they are trying to steal horses, or sneak into unwatched private residences,*

or are filling the air with their drunken brawls. The worst elements of the
great army are here in their worst condition; its cowards, its thieves, its sneaks,
its bullying vagabonds, all inflamed with whiskey.[118]

Frederick, like other cities and towns in Maryland, never succeeded in reining in soldiers who were determined to avoid their duties and escape from the eyes of the authorities. On a single night there in March 1864, at least sixty-three men were in the guardhouse for intoxication. There were many times when drunken soldiers were not captured before they did serious damage. Mr. William Exner, a young man on his way home in the evening, was assaulted by a party of inebriated soldiers and "beaten in the most shocking manner." Other citizens intervened in Exner's behalf, and the cowardly offenders then ran away from the scene.[119]

The trains coming from Washington passing through Baltimore brought what the *Sun* called "the usual quota of intoxicated men, who very frequently straggle behind, fall down on the sidewalks," and create problems for themselves and the civilians on the streets. The newspaper noted that since they had just been paid, the police were keeping their money for safekeeping until they were sober. There were incidents when soldiers walked into bars and the owner or bartender refused to serve them because it was against military regulations. Sergeant George Greer, from the Thirteenth Pennsylvania, went into the Mount Clare House, demanded a drink and then shot the owner in the face for refusal to comply. A similar incident occurred in Canton when soldiers were denied whiskey. They proceeded to assault Mrs. Menger, knock her down, beat her in the face and sprain her wrist. Not content with the personal attack on the woman, they continued their destruction by battering the furniture in the beer house.[120] On nearby Eastern Avenue in Baltimore City, a fight broke out one night between 5:00 and 6:00 p.m. involving both soldiers and citizens that was caused, according to the *Baltimore Clipper*, "by whiskey and lewd women."[121] A tragic event on July 9, 1864, occurred in Sandy Hook, where drunken soldiers on horseback were galloping through the narrow streets of the town: "A curious little girl, attracted by the noise, got too close to the inebriated soldiers and was accidently shot and killed."[122]

A number of astute observers noted that the alcohol problem in the military was made all the more difficult because the officers often failed to set the proper example. Charles H. Russell, of the First Maryland Cavalry stationed at Fort Carroll, wrote to his friend Ward Lamon about his commander, a Lieutenant Colonel Miller, who was so drunk that he was unable to stay in his saddle to lead them through morning drills. This was

Scenes of punishment for misbehavior. *Library of Congress.*

Liquor brought by an African American servant to officers. *Library of Congress.*

a chronic problem. Russell complained, "One thing makes me unpopular around here—viz., I will not curse, drink & whore with the majority of the officers."[123] Osceola Lewis, a member of the 138th Pennsylvania Volunteer Regiment guarding the B&O Railroad, boasted about the strict discipline of his unit and the cordial relationship between the soldiers and civilians in the area. However, he indicated that there were grave problems with one of the officers. According to Lewis, Colonel Charles L.K. Sumwalt was dismissed from the service for his behavior: "He became addicted to drunkenness and lost all sense of shame, honor or manly dignity."[124] Drunkenness and misbehavior among soldiers of rank became so prevalent in Baltimore that Major General Wallace issued an order in October 1864 that officers were not permitted to go into the city during their free time unless they had specific authorization from his headquarters.[125] Their failure to set standards invariably contributed to demoralization of their enlisted men.

The Union military authorities tried a number of approaches to reduce the occurrence of drunkenness involving officers and enlisted men. Guards were sent to taverns violating the rules in a number of towns and cities, and they emptied huge quantities of alcohol into the streets. In Baltimore, the provost marshal routinely handled most of the cases involving the sale of liquor to soldiers, imposing a fine or imprisonment for those responsible. That policy changed in March 1864 with the announcement that offenders of the regulations would be immediately imprisoned to await trial by a military commission. In his jurisdiction, Brigadier General E.B. Tyler used a different tactic. He issued a General Order in June 1864 that anyone selling liquor to government employees would receive all the punishments outlined previously, plus "confinement on bread and water, hard labor, with ball and chain, or fine not exceeding $100."[126] On Maryland's Eastern Shore in early 1862, Brigadier General Lockwood ordered that anyone selling liquor within the limits of his command would be punished with one month of labor or a month of prison with only bread and water. Lockwood explained in his General Orders No. 1 that it was almost impossible to sell alcohol to troops without "great abuse." None of these measures succeeded in a significant reduction of the problem. Indeed, the violations of orders continued until the end of the war and afterward. People were arrested after Lincoln's assassination for not closing their taverns until his funeral was over. In May 1865, four soldiers who were drunk in the streets of Baltimore attacked another soldier, some citizens who came to his aid and the policemen who arrived to arrest them.[127]

The occupation of Maryland resulted in the rise to a new class of individuals: the enablers, those determined to profit in some manner by taking advantage of the soldiers. They served liquor in their taverns, sold civilian clothes to deserters to facilitate their escape and charged exorbitant prices for their merchandise. They waited until the hapless men were inattentive or asleep to take advantage of them. The enablers stole food from wounded soldiers and cheated enlistees out of their bounties. In every town and city in Maryland where the soldiers came, they met these enablers and often were the victims of their scams. On May 29, 1865, the *Sun* reported that no fewer than six hundred soldiers were in the guardhouse. They editorialized, "Nearly all this trouble is produced by unprincipled persons, who sell them drugged or poisonous drinks that a better opportunity may be offered to rob them of money and valuables."[128] The Reverend Alonzo Quint, chaplain for the Second Massachusetts Infantry, then located near Frederick, found it difficult to believe that the "power which sends men to Fort Lafayette by mere executive warrant" would not be able to deal with the liquor vendors that defy military orders and sell to the soldiers.[129]

Some enablers were repeat offenders. In Baltimore, H.H. Dixon was caught three times selling alcohol to soldiers, and by the third offense, he was spending thirty days in a military prison. In Frederick, Mr. Eckstein's bar was closed, and all his liquor was confiscated after his third violation of the law. After bar owner John Oates was arrested for the third time, the *Frederick Examiner* weighed in on this subject: "The reprehensible practice of selling liquor to soldiers is the source of much disorder and infringement of discipline, and ought to be interdicted in the most rigorous manner." The most egregious offenders often did end up in military prison, as was the case of John C. Myers and Daniel Henry in Baltimore. Eastern Avenue in the city was lined with taverns whose owners repeatedly violated military regulations. On one night in November 1864, seven women and two men were arrested there and charged with selling alcohol to soldiers.[130]

Enablers appeared in many guises, were of all ages and both sexes and were typically open to any opportunities to enrich themselves. James Daynes of Baltimore, who was only a boy at the time, was locked up in military prison pending a hearing for selling liquor to soldiers. Mrs. Bridget Hogan was arrested by authorities for selling liquor to soldiers, drugging them, peddling civilian clothing to military personnel and aiding them in deserting. Emma Crothers was arrested in a brothel for robbing John Sherlock, of the 159th Regiment of Ohio Volunteers, of $40. George Stewart visited homes in two wards in Baltimore, telling prospective draftees that he could

Two soldiers with liquor and cards. *Library of Congress.*

relieve them of their military obligation if they paid him. After he collected money, he was promptly arrested. Alexander Telly was picked up by the police after stealing $105 from a soldier who fell asleep in Lexington Market. The provost marshal's office, aware of scammers selling their wares in the vicinity of the Soldiers' Rest Rooms, ordered all the merchants in the area to close permanently. Major General Lew Wallace, commanding the Middle Department, explained, "This stringent order has been issued on account of the alleged abuses which some of the proprietors have practiced on soldiers." Some of those selling goods had inflated the prices, charging $125 for a suit worth only $25, and $10 for a watch that was then stolen back. Some of the items sold contained whiskey, and some of the storekeepers were allowing soldiers to use their stores to change into civilian clothes and then desert. The provost marshal felt compelled to mandate that anyone conducting further business in the area would have his goods confiscated, and the items taken would be distributed to sick and wounded soldiers.[131]

One of the most tragic cases of enabling involved a prostitute and a Union soldier, the latter arriving at Camden Station dead inside a trunk. Margaret Louisa Linder, who described herself to the police as a person of "bad repute," had fallen in love with Samuel Freeborn of the New York cavalry. Sick and tired of the war, he devised a scheme to desert from the Union army in Norfolk by concealing himself in a trunk with air holes and a canteen. She had the chest put on a steamer and traveled with him up the Chesapeake Bay to Baltimore. Unfortunately, when she opened the trunk, she found her beloved dead from suffocation, and in a state of panic, she left him at the station. This "mysterious affair" intrigued both the press and the general public for days. Later, devastated by the outcome and desolate without her lover, she went to the police station in tears to confess her role in this scheme. Although not guilty of murder, she was arrested for aiding a deserter and then tried.[132]

The institution of the draft provided additional opportunities for war profiteers in Maryland. In Baltimore, brokers were defrauding men who had signed up as substitutes out of their bounties. Out of fifty recent recruits in late August 1864, not one had received the bounty they had been promised. In a similar scheme to make money, five men were arrested for running substitutes into Delaware and with furnishing existing soldiers with civilian clothes so they could desert and become substitutes in that state. Mr. Hiss, a justice of the peace, caused quite a scandal when he and two others were arrested and put in military prison, "charged with compelling colored men to enter the army as substitutes." John Starr, in a similar crime, was caught kidnapping African Americans at gunpoint and then selling them as substitutes.[133] Civilians and soldiers were both involved in schemes such as the selling and purchasing of U.S. military blankets, muskets and even horses.

Many attempts to reduce or alleviate the problems associated with enabling were unsuccessful. A common tactic was to destroy the enabler's enticement and then humiliate the offender. In Annapolis, the provost guard went to a bar on State Circle and destroyed $1,500 worth of liquor and bar fixtures. In Baltimore, on October 5, 1863, five proprietors of liquor establishments were arrested, and all of their inventories (twenty-one barrels in total) were taken. They were told to stand in the streets with signs around their necks declaring, "I sell liquor to soldiers." A few days later, three men were ordered to complete the same punishment by parading with placards on Baltimore Street, where apparently they attracted a large crowd of men, women and children who enjoyed the spectacle considerably. In Frederick, six establishments were closed for selling liquor; some were heavily fined, and others were forbidden to ever reopen. One proprietor was compelled to stand on a box with a sign reading, "I buy whiskey for soldiers." In Hagerstown, the provost marshal's office issued an order that if drunken soldiers were loitering in the vicinity of an establishment, the authorities would assume that the proprietors were responsible for serving them, and arrests and closures would follow.[134] Throughout the state, these enablers filled the jail cells, cost the military time and resources and contributed to dereliction of duty on the part of both enlisted men and their officers. The enablers were war profiteers—men and women who used the weaknesses and vulnerabilities of the soldiers to enrich their coffers. Ironically, many were unionists, individuals who seemed blissfully ignorant or unconcerned about their inadvertent undermining of the Federal war effort.

5

United States Colored Troops, Free Blacks and Slaves

We are Union men from principle, uncompromising Union men, opposed to
Emancipation Disunion as well as Secession Disunion.
—Easton Gazette, *January 3, 1863*

When the men of the Twenty-first New York Regiment arrived in Baltimore in June 1861, they carried loaded muskets because of their distrust of the secessionists in the city. According to their regimental historian, the local women stared at them with scowling and hateful faces. When the men offered them oranges and other fruits, the soldiers declined because they had heard rumors about the possibility of being poisoned by the Rebel sympathizers. According to J. Harrison Mills, "the loyalty of the darkeys, however, was unquestionable, and we did not hesitate to buy of them what they chose to bring for our refreshment."[135] This observation by Mills reflected an assumption that the future of African Americans was linked in some way with the Federal cause. Not all soldiers or civilians would have agreed with him at the onset of the Civil War, but the entire socioeconomic system based on slave labor was under assault and would crumble by 1865.

The Union war effort in Maryland and elsewhere was more problematic because of a lack of agreement on the part of both the military and civilians over the purposes for fighting. At the beginning of the war, Federal soldiers often made a concerted effort to return runaway slaves to their owners. One escapee found in a military camp located just south of Hagerstown was sent back to the owner in the Clear Spring District. In another incident in

Washington County, a slave of Mrs. Philip Schindel presented himself as a free man to an officer of one of the Pennsylvania regiments; the officer voluntarily returned the man to bondage when he found out the truth. When the Fourth Connecticut Regiment came through Frederick, it also reunited a runaway with Mr. Samuel Horine, the slaveholder.[136] This policy, initially conciliatory to Maryland's landed gentry and political elite, would rapidly change during the course of the conflict.

When Lincoln issued the preliminary Emancipation Proclamation, it was apparent that his war aims had broadened beyond the salvation of the Union to encompass freedom for those in bondage. Although the president's proclamation was issued officially on January 1, 1863, as a war measure, it applied only to those areas not under Federal control. Maryland, as a border state that remained in the Union, was not covered by Lincoln's declaration, so slavery continued in the state until the ratification of a new Constitution in 1864 that abolished the institution. Since those who refused to take the oath of allegiance were generally disqualified from voting, most of the voices heard on this issue were unionists and Maryland's Union soldiers, who had been given permission to vote in the field. The majority of Maryland's civilians opposed the new Constitution, but the soldiers' vote in favor was enough for passage by the extremely narrow margin of 299 votes.[137] The closeness of the vote was partially a reflection of divisions within the Union Party, and it was also an expression of the stubborn reluctance of some residents to relinquish their servants and field hands or to alter a social hierarchy that placed African Americans on the bottom. Resentment over the abolition of slavery and the arming of free blacks and slaves fueled more prejudice, harassment and violence against blacks in Maryland during the Civil War. White civilians and Union forces saw slaves, free blacks and the United States Colored Troops (USCT) as symbols of what the war promised: the destruction of an institution that dated back to ancient times and a dramatic transformation of race relations.

Racial violence started early in the war and continued long after it terminated, and it was present in all regions of the state. In Washington County, in western Maryland, Captain Isaac T. Prather, who was recruiting for USCT, was shot in Hagerstown by a paroled soldier who had been assaulting black recruits. In Dorchester County on Maryland's Eastern Shore, a soldier from the USCT, recently discharged because of battle wounds, was the center of attention at a party thrown in his honor. A constable and three other white men arrived uninvited, assaulted and drove away the guests at the event and then badly beat the black soldier.[138] The assailants involved in this episode were arrested, although there were other cases of white violence against blacks that were not prosecuted by authorities.

The routine of everyday life in the state was punctuated by such attacks that deliberately targeted African Americans. A black soldier, apparently a straggler, was walking on the streets of Baltimore when he was accosted by two white soldiers from the Third Maryland Cavalry, one of whom picked up a brick and allegedly bashed in the nose and the head of the member of the USCT. A similar event occurred in this city when a soldier and a civilian were charged with assaulting USCT soldiers; both were arrested and jailed. In a separate incident, white soldiers attacked black soldiers in the street, and one of the latter was severely beaten.[139] In February 1864, two companies of USCT escorted about fifty African American recruits from Anne Arundel County through the streets of Baltimore. Despite the armed guards, several soldiers from Maryland regiments watching the procession hurled epithets and bricks at the marching men.[140]

One of the largest and most unfathomable events of racial violence occurred in 1863, when convalescent troops coming from Philadelphia and waiting in railroad cars decided to cause mayhem on the streets of Baltimore. As the *Sun* noted: "Quite an excitement was created on Pratt Street yesterday morning by an indiscriminate attack on colored people by a body of about two hundred soldiers." The men left their train, got brickbats and began an unprovoked assault on black draymen and laborers who were about to start their work early in the morning. They pursued every African American in sight, vandalized and invaded their homes and broke windows. When the police arrived, they were attacked as they tried to quell the riot.[141]

Racial turmoil was nothing new, but the decision to arm African Americans was very difficult for many Marylanders to accept and just accentuated tensions between the two races. The *Frederick Examiner*, a staunchly unionist voice, spoke for many when it expressed alarm in 1862 at the practice of officers in some Union camps allowing their black servants or camp followers to be uniformed and sometimes armed. The editors declared, "This practice cannot fail to be demoralizing to the soldiers, as it is corrupting to the servants in private families. We would also remark that the laws of the state prohibit negroes from carrying or having fire-arms, nevertheless, we are told, that the negro army servants occasionally wear pistols in the street."[142] The debate regarding both emancipation and blacks in uniform was heated both on the homefront and in the field.

Frederick W. Wild from Alexander's Baltimore Battery of Light Artillery, when captured by the Confederates en route to Gettysburg, had an interesting

Black and white soldiers defended the Constitution. *Harper's Weekly.*

conversation with a "Johnnie" from North Carolina about the objectives of the war. "I told him we were fighting for the maintenance of the Union, and not to free the negroes, much less make them masters of white men; even if it would be necessary to free the negroes to save the Union, the land and other property would not be taken from the white people." Wild believed that he had much in common with the North Carolinian because the latter was a unionist but joined the Confederate army over the issue of slavery.[143] There were some unionists in Maryland, just like Wild, who were hoping for some way to avoid freeing and arming the black population. One of these was Maryland's governor, Thomas Hicks, who personally went to the Naval Academy grounds in Annapolis in October 1861 to demand that the soldiers return one of his runaway slaves. Not only did they fail to cooperate, but also the escapee, who had been hiding in a chimney, was provided a boat to row away from the city.[144] Less than a year later, in July 1862, Maryland and the other border states rejected Lincoln's proposal for compensated emancipation. The *Easton Gazette*, a unionist publication, strongly supported the state's decision, arguing that Marylanders had already sacrificed enough for the war effort. In their view: "The right to hold slaves is a right appertaining to all of the States of the Union. They have the right to cherish or abolish the institution."[145] But the exigencies of war were far outpacing the evolution of opinion on this subject.

Sergeant Major Christian Fleetwood, a Baltimorean and Medal of Honor winner from the Fourth USCT, wrote, "The North came slowly and reluctantly to recognize the Negro as a factor for good in the war. 'This is a white man's war,' met the Negroes at every step of their efforts to gain admission to the armies of the Union." Fleetwood gave most of the credit for the recognition of the value of African American troops to Major General David Hunter. The latter was called before Congress to explain why he armed some African Americans in his command in the spring of 1862. His speech regarding the value of these men to the war efforts was greeted with scorn and laughter, according to Fleetwood.[146]

A prominent Maryland opponent of the arming of African Americans was Congressman Henry May, who delivered a speech on the subject in the House of Representatives in 1863. May explained: "Sir, we who recognize the amiable disposition of the domesticated African, his inert nature, his slovenly habits, his clumsiness, his want of vigilance, and his timidity, know that of all human beings, he presents the least qualifications for a soldier."[147] On the other side of the question were Unconditional Unionists, who were members of the faction of the Union Party that dominated Maryland

Christian Fleetwood, Baltimorean and Medal of Honor recipient. *Library of Congress.*

Frederick Douglass lobbying for enlistment of black soldiers. *Library of Congress.*

politics during the latter part of the war. U.S. House member Henry Winter Davis, for example, supported emancipation and later suffrage for African Americans. In a speech in Philadelphia in 1863, he maintained that recruiting black soldiers would lead to freedom for the slaves and additional strength for the Union forces. Davis asserted, "You will have wrested the sword from your antagonist, and will wield it over his defenseless head." In the following year, Davis made a cogent argument in the House of Representatives that slavery anywhere in the nation was "really radically inconsistent with the permanence of republican institutions."[148]

Frederick Douglass, a very influential Maryland-born activist, was the most prominent and eloquent spokesman on behalf of enlisting slaves. When the Confederates fired on Fort Sumter in 1861, he predicted that the war would not be fought solely with white soldiers, and he then became an early advocate of arming the black man to suppress the twin evils of slavery and rebellion. In his papers "Men of Color, To Arms" and "Why the Colored Man Should Enlist," he argued that "the arm of the slave was the best defense against the arm of the slave-holder." Douglass, whose two sons, Charles and Lewis, enlisted in Massachusetts regiments, urged others to do the same. He told his audience that morality dictated that a man do what was right, that military service was one of the sacred duties of citizenship and that it would provide dignity and pride to a people who had been told they were deficient in courage. Rights were not secured primarily through persuasion, but through actions, and gaining proficiency in arms would enable blacks to defend themselves and their freedoms in the future. Douglass maintained that secessionists, who love slavery and hate the Negro, regarded the idea of arming blacks as a "calamity" and were doing their utmost to prevent such an occurrence.[149]

Dr. Alexander T. Augusta, another pioneering civil rights leader and former Maryland resident, played a significant role in the history and advancement of African Americans in the Civil War. Born a free man in Virginia in 1825, he moved to Baltimore in the 1840s to become a journeyman barber, a step toward his goal of becoming a physician. After studying under private tutors in the city, he sought admission into the University of Pennsylvania medical school but was denied because of his race. Eventually, Augusta secured his medical degree, but only by moving to Canada and studying in Toronto. He returned to the United States in 1862, when he sought and secured a surgeon's commission as a major from President Lincoln and was placed for a time at Camp Staunton in Benedict, Maryland, where recruits for the Seventh United States Colored Troops were training. Augusta's experiences there and elsewhere were testimony to the prevalence of discrimination in the military. Despite the fact that he was the highest-ranking black officer, the paymaster in Baltimore insisted on wages of seven dollars a month, after the clothing deduction. Augusta, as senior surgeon in camp, found that white doctors were unwilling to work under him or take orders from him. His assistants wrote a letter of protest to Lincoln expressing their shock at Augusta's position and asking for his "termination" in a relationship they found offensive. They stated in their letter, "But we cannot…willingly compromise what we consider a proper self-respect, nor do we deem that the interests of either the country or of the colored race, can demand this of us."[150] In 1863, Major Augusta was the victim of racial violence in a riot at President Street Station in Baltimore. A huge crowd gathered there, seeing him in an officer's uniform, assaulted him until men from the provost marshal's office arrived. Even with the presence of these armed guards, Augusta was attacked again as he was escorted to his train.[151]

Despite the racial prejudice of those who objected to any use of black troops, on July 6, 1863, Maryland, once the home of Alexander Augusta, Frederick Douglass and Harriet Tubman, received authorization to begin forming units of the United States Colored Troops. This action would culminate eventually in the creation of six full regiments—the Fourth, Seventh, Ninth, Nineteenth, Thirtieth and Thirty-ninth—and in total, the state contributed 8,700 African American males to the Federal army.[152] While the initial decision was to enlist free men only, some recruiters went beyond their mandate and actively recruited slaves. In July 1863, Colonel William Birney visited Mr. Campbell's Negro Jail in Baltimore, where owners had sent their slaves for safekeeping. Birney freed all the inmates and then encouraged them to enlist. J.P. Creager, a Union recruiter for Carroll and Frederick Counties, caused quite a stir in those jurisdictions by enrolling slaves at sites like Bethel Church and Asbury Chapel Graveyard in Frederick. He admitted that he did not ask whether they were free or slave. After one slaveholder took the matter to court, a posse was formed, and Creager was arrested. Brigadier General Morris eventually suspended him from his duties because of this controversy.[153]

Continuing huge losses in the Union army due to disease, death and desertion led the War Department to approve the enrollment of slaves in the border states. Maryland began to implement this policy in October 1863, and nineteen recruiting stations were established.[154] For those slaveholders who lost what they considered their "property" in this manner, it was a bitter blow. Initially, slaveholders supporting the Union were required to consent to recruitment of their slaves; however, if quotas were not reached within thirty days, their agreement was unnecessary. Owners were required to prove loyalty, provide a manumission deed and file a claim to be compensated the $100 to $300 for each slave, depending on how much time was left on the individual's term of bondage. Secessionists who had slaves received nothing for their loss.

President Lincoln expected resistance to this policy, and that was indeed the case in Maryland. In a letter on October 21, 1863, to Major General Robert Schenck, the president wrote the following: "A delegation is here saying that our armed colored troops are at many, if not all, the landings on the Patuxent River, and by their presence with arms in their hands are frightening quiet people, and producing great confusion. Have they been sent there by any

Contrabands (fugitive slaves) passed through Maryland to get north of the Mason-Dixon line. *Library of Congress.*

order, and if so, for what reason?" Schenck responded that the USCT had been camping and recruiting there when two rabid secessionists murdered a Union officer. The president told him to come at once to discuss this matter and added, "It might be better to send white recruiters."[155] This particular incident involved the slaying of Lieutenant Eben White and the wounding of a private from the Seventh USCT when they went to the plantation of Colonel John Sothoron and his son, both fanatical Southern sympathizers.[156] As a result of this event, an officer was sent down to Point Lookout to gather a force to return with him to restore order and to secure a gunboat to prevent the owners from running their slaves from Maryland into Virginia.[157]

Another episode entailing local opposition occurred in Easton. Major Samuel Kramer, of the Third Maryland Regiment, was sent to the Eastern

African American soldiers in training. *Harper's Weekly.*

Shore to recruit blacks. There he found approximately fifty men, mostly farm hands, who were willing to enlist. But when the men went down to the wharf to get onboard the steamer, outraged slave owners came and threatened all of those involved. Kramer told the captain of the steamer to depart immediately, and as he did so, "the chagrined and mortified rebels stood gazing in mute astonishment at the receding boat, bearing off 'their servants' as they called them."[158] This type of incident did not deter the continued formation of African American regiments, and by March 1864 in St. Mary's County, recruiters had taken a "veritable stampede" of one thousand slaves and many free blacks from owners and employers and left on ships for Fortress Monroe.[159] These changes to the socioeconomic status quo happened too quickly for many whites in the state and were certainly a source of much anger and simmering resentment. In a short period of time, the Union authorities had transformed slaves from "property" to valuable assets for winning the war.

Those blacks remaining at home were in danger from both their white neighbors and from Union soldiers. In Frederick, the African American community had little recourse when racial injustice or violence occurred, as happened so frequently, according to the *Examiner*:

> *For some time past the colored population of this city has been subject to a system of abuse or outrage. It seems the soldiers or persons dressed in U.S. uniforms have made it their business under cover of night to maltreat and knock down old and decrepit negro men and women, together with the perpetuation of other outrages.*[160]

African Americans, in Frederick and elsewhere, became convenient scapegoats for all that seemed to be wrong with the war.

Racism was widespread in both North and South and was prevalent among many of the men in the Union army stationed in Maryland. The Reverend Alonzo Quint, a chaplain with the Second Massachusetts, located at Camp Hicks north of Frederick, commented on the segregation at the Baptist church in town. He noted, "It has, of course, a negro gallery, entirely separating the black from the white Christians…It is very comforting to know that, by this arrangement, there is no possible danger of contamination."[161] John Mead Gould, guarding the B&O Railroad with the Tenth Maine, was a strong supporter of General McClellan, in part because he opposed the "purpose of bringing the everlasting nigger into the war."[162] William Combs, a soldier in the Fourteenth New Hampshire stationed in Poolesville near the

C&O Canal, told his wife in a letter that African Americans did not want to be free. He also observed that he would like to live in Maryland, but he did not want the "damd nigers" because he hated them more than the devil. Combs, like many soldiers who wrote about race in their letters and diaries, did not see any need to provide rationalizations for views that were so ubiquitous in nineteenth-century America.[163]

Many citizens on both sides perceived the state's African Americans, whether free or slave, through vision clouded with stereotypes and misconceptions. Union soldiers commonly made blacks objects of ridicule or comedy. Andrew E. Ford, of the Fifteenth Massachusetts Regiment, when discussing what they did for amusement in camp at Poolesville, mentioned possum hunts, cards and catching flying squirrels. He added: "The universal darkey was the source of unlimited fun."[164] Leverett Bradley, of the First Massachusetts Heavy Artillery, camped on Maryland Heights, wrote in a letter to his family about the soldiers securing black persons to dance as entertainment when the darkness came early in November. He noted, "as long as the music lasts, we have a great deal of sport with them."[165] In Pleasant Valley, after the Battle of Antietam, men from the Sixth New Hampshire Regiment deliberately targeted some black children who were working for the troops at their camp. When some of the soldiers saw the chaplain teaching the young boys to read, they resented this. Determined to express their displeasure by having some fun at the expense of the children, they waited until the boys were sitting in a covered wagon and then shoved it down a long hill until it crashed at the bottom; fortunately, no one was hurt. One of the men in the regiment explained that this episode happened in 1862, "before the soldiers learned to respect duly the colored man's rights."[166]

For many Union soldiers coming into Maryland from north of the Mason-Dixon line, the sight of African Americans—whether free, slave or soldier—was a novel one. Some had no previous personal contact with blacks and thus often reacted to them based on what they had heard and read about race relations prior to their enlistment. Upon their arrival in Annapolis, soldiers of the Third New Hampshire Infantry received a grim introduction to the horrors attendant to slavery when they beheld the sight of a female slave hanging from a gallows for the crime of poisoning her master.[167] Northern troops stationed on the Eastern Shore may have heard about or witnessed the lynching in Queenstown of a slave for impregnating a seventeen-year-old white girl.[168] Herbert Valentine of the Twenty-third Massachusetts Volunteers mentioned that while in camp in Annapolis, we made "out first acquaintance with the negroes…Here we first heard their

African American workers, possibly at the Giesboro cavalry depot. *Library of Congress.*

strange wild melodies, sung with infinite zest and abandon, telling in their minor strains and weird cadences the sad story of bondage."[169] Stephen G. Abbott, chaplain of the First New Hampshire Regiment, was interested in the racial attitudes of Marylanders and found them very sensitive on issues relating to slavery and determinedly adverse to any Yankee influence on this matter. While in camp in Dawsonville, Abbott met a young lady and asked her to correspond with him, and she did so until the issue of the Emancipation Proclamation was raised. In the chaplain's words: "Union and Emancipation meant very different things to the people of Maryland." He also received a letter from a very staunch unionist supporter requesting that the New Hampshire men, if they wished to save the nation, should cease interfering with the slaves.[170] Francis Buffum, of the Fourteenth New Hampshire Volunteers, described race relations in Maryland during the first part of the war as "anomalous and perplexing" and found that "the presence of the Union troops aggravated the difficulty of the situation. There was a general uneasiness; and the puzzled slave not only dared not to express his sentiments, but was fearful of having any sentiments."[171]

As far as Maryland's Union soldiers were concerned, the majority voted in favor of the new 1864 Constitution for a wide variety of reasons but primarily because they strongly supported President Lincoln, who had linked emancipation with the salvation of the Union as joint war objectives. Many Federals had fought under a banner of "Union and Freedom" from the official declaration of the Emancipation Proclamation on January 1, 1863, until the voting on the Maryland Constitution in the fall of 1864. Liberating the state's slaves was in a sense both a payoff and the natural byproduct of the victories and sacrifices of all men in the Union army during this period. The acceptance of African American troops by white Federal soldiers increased with the progression of the war as USCT soldiers proved their martial skills, courage on the battlefield and willingness to put their own lives in jeopardy.

But there were some in the military who remained unconvinced about the wisdom of either emancipation or arming blacks. Robert Kirkwood, of the First Maryland Regiment, expressed the following about using African American labor on behalf of the Union cause:

> *There is great dissatisfaction in camp* [Maryland Heights] *about the President's Proclamation. They think he is carrying thing*[s] *a little to*[o] *far as it regards employing to work on fortifications. I am for it but when they come to putting arms into their hands and fighting with them I will ask Mr. Lincoln to take my place.*[172]

Captain E.W. Moffett in a letter to his father on January 20, 1863, from the headquarters of the Eighth Regiment Maryland Volunteers, also expressed his displeasure with the Lincoln administration. He wrote that it had "forgotten the Cause that the War was for. I have not if they have. I think it was one for the Restoration of the Union and not for Abolishing slavery which it has come to."[173] Some in the military retained their antagonism as they returned home and found a difficult transition to peacetime. Thomas Monroe, a Union soldier working at the U.S. general hospital in Frederick right after the war ended, remarked in a letter to friends in June 1865 that it was hard for a white man to find a job because blacks were willing to work for lower wages. He bemoaned the fact that Federal troops "have fought and sufered [*sic*] everything in defence of their country and to free the slaves that now they should take Bread out of their mouths to feed the Blacks and now the negroes are not satisfied." Instead, he said, they were demanding the right to vote.[174]

The sights of United States Colored Troops in the streets or of African Americans celebrating the passage of the 1864 Constitution were painful to behold for many whites. Dr. Thomas Frances Johnson of Baltimore, soon after the new document was implemented, wrote to William Johnson about his feelings on this subject. "We are all getting on here pretty much as usual under the rule of the soldiers and their friends—the Darkies have taken complete possession of our city since the new Constitution came to light kicking up their heels in joy over the glorious event."[175] This identification of the Union with abolitionism and the possible enfranchisement of blacks heightened partisan divisions in Maryland and were factors in the resurgence of the Democratic Party in the state after the war ended. Manumitting and empowering African Americans were risky political ventures, and both contributed to the unremitting persecution and violence against this minority.

Major General John Gibbon, after serving as one of the commissioners accepting the surrender of Lee's Army of Northern Virginia, returned to his wife in Baltimore and commented on the state of race relations at the end of the war. In a letter to Mr. Latrobe on September 1865, he indicated that the temper of the people was much better than he expected but that the future of African Americans in Maryland remained problematic. He wrote, "They are lazy and disinclined to work, and the mischief of it is that the negro question is a delicate one to handle without burning one's fingers in these ticklish twins of freedom and free suffrage!"[176] Many white Marylanders, both unionists and secessionists, agreed with this viewpoint and were not willing to make the transition to a new social and political order.

6

Secessionists in Jeopardy

Again treason has been so very respectable in Maryland—so aristocratic…that it
is time it should be branded as a disgrace.[177]
—*Dr. Samuel Harrison*

Madge Preston, a woman who lived on a plantation just outside Baltimore City, penned a short message in her diary on March 9, 1864. In it she said, "I was greatly annoyed today by a troop of colored soldiers coming to the house to get recruits on the place."[178] Mrs. Preston, an avowed secessionist, dreaded the appearance in her area of either black or white Union soldiers. Like many supporters of the South, her perspective on the military occupation vacillated between fear and annoyance. Martha Elizabeth Harris of Leonardtown expressed similar consternation in her diary on March 30, 1863: "Soldiers among us, causing mischief, searching houses, destroying everything they touch, interfering with our servants."[179] These women, and other residents who sympathized with the South, were in clear and present danger from their Union occupiers. If they became active in war-related activities, they faced possible in-home arrest, incarceration, confiscation of property or even execution. Many of the offenders were exiled to the South, to the north of Philadelphia or even to the Dry Tortugas islands in the Gulf of Mexico.

The percentage of Marylanders who identified with the Southern cause was unknown; however, there were a number of indicators that the state was predominately unionist, including that fact that there was about a three-to-one ratio of Union enlistments to Confederate ones. At a Union Party meeting in Baltimore, one of the resolutions adopted stated: "That while one-third of the people of Maryland are false to their allegiance, two-thirds of her people are loyal to the government of their fathers."[180] The vast majority of Union soldiers, in their letters, journals, diaries and regimental histories, observed that they felt very warmly supported here, although it was not uncommon to encounter a "secesh" in their travels, particularly on the Eastern Shore, in southern Maryland and in Baltimore. The landed gentry were well represented in the ranks of civilian Rebels, while German and Irish immigrants and the native-born working class tended to fall in the Federal camp. Rapid industrialization and the transportation revolution were creating a burgeoning mercantile class with strong commercial ties to the North, although Maryland also had cultural affinities with the South, particularly in relation to slavery. The state's political elite was divided in allegiance. While some Southern-sympathizing state legislators were arrested early in the war, Maryland had three wartime governors who were unionists, as were such well-known leaders as John Pendleton Kennedy and Reverdy Johnson.

The Federal authorities stationed in Maryland, aware of the state's divided loyalties, were extremely harsh in their treatment of the secessionists, so much so that the punishments that they meted out were in a number of cases overturned by the president or the War Department. In 1864, a military commission in Baltimore sentenced four men to death by hanging because they were found to be Rebel spies, blockade runners or mail carriers. The president commuted their sentences.[181] Likewise, Lincoln ordered the release of Sarah Hutchins from incarceration a little over a month after a military commission in Baltimore sentenced her to five years in Fitchburg Prison in Massachusetts. She was accused of treason for a number of crimes, including purchasing an elegant sword for dashing Confederate cavalryman and local hero Colonel Harry Gilmor.[182] Teenage spy and mail courier Sallie Pollock of Cumberland was also released early from her sentence by military commission to the penitentiary in Pittsburgh. When Major General David Hunter developed a blacklist of Southern supporters and decided to expel many of them across the Potomac, the War Department suspended his orders. Surprisingly, in Frederick, Provost Marshal Yellott rearrested those on the list, then released them on a $3,000 bond each and required them to report to his office every morning.[183]

At times when martial law was declared, the secessionists were on the defensive. During the Gettysburg campaign, Major General Schenck

The grave of Sallie Pollock, Confederate spy and mail courier, along the C&O Canal.
Author's photo.

issued an order that no citizens in Baltimore City or County were permitted to possess weapons unless they were enrolled as volunteers. Soldiers spread out through the area and searched houses, confiscating muskets, pistols, rifles and swords.[184] These weapons seized in July were not returned to loyal civilians until October, but secessionists were not allowed to reclaim their arms even if they could prove ownership. Some perceived this as a clear violation of the Second Amendment, but in wartime, they had little recourse.

There were other possible hardships that Confederate sympathizers faced: they could not vote unless they took the oath of allegiance; in Baltimore City and some other jurisdictions, they were barred from certain professions like teaching or working for the government; and their businesses could be closed at any time if they promoted treasonous ideas or commodities. In the Military District of the Patuxent, a jurisdiction that encompassed three counties in the state, the headquarters issued an order at the end of the war that no one could engage in an occupation or profession if they refused to take an oath of allegiance.[185] Maryland farmers who harbored secessionist sympathies faced an additional threat if Union troops in the area were aware of their proclivities. George C. Gordon, of the Twenty-fourth Michigan Infantry, who was in Maryland after the Battle of Antietam, confessed in a letter that they deliberately retaliated against supporters of the enemy. "We pick out the secesh sympathizers for that purpose and let 30–40 thousand troops camp on a plantation and fence rails melt like a frost in June. Straw ditto."[186] Retaliation took many forms. When the men of the Seventy-third Ohio Volunteer Infantry were camped between Middletown and South Mountain, they got incensed over the high prices they were charged for goods by Southern sympathizers living nearby, and "from this cause, doubtless, arose the rumor that their chickens rested poorly of nights and their potatoes were not likely to take a second growth."[187] When the Duryee Zouaves first arrived in Baltimore, some of the men went to the known secessionist neighborhoods and refused to let any citizens on the sidewalks. They either had to walk in the street, go back in their houses or be knocked down by the soldiers.[188] These harassing tactics were clearly a way to declare their mastery over the sector of the population that was unsupportive.

Words, symbols and actions of secessionists were punishable if they were in any way indicative of anti-Union partisanship. On June 25, 1863, at the corner of Greenmount and Eager Streets in Baltimore, three young men cheered for Jefferson Davis and Stonewall Jackson. When the provost guard arrived to stop them, there was a scuffle and a shooting. Although no one was hurt, the civilians were arrested. Cheering for Davis also led to the arrests of Anne Nugent, Mary R. Murphy and Mary L. Moore on April 28, 1864. In Frederick, Mrs. J.W. Heard displayed a secessionist headdress out her window, so the provost marshal seized it. Soldiers searched the residence of J.M. Kunkle, a prominent Frederick lawyer, where they uncovered a secessionist flag, pictures of Jefferson Davis and General Beauregard and memorabilia of other noteworthy Confederates. An informer reported to the provost marshal's office in Baltimore that Mrs. Betts on North Calvert Street had a Rebel flag draped on her chandelier, so soldiers came and removed it. Any "emblem of treason," no matter how small or trivial, was fair game for the authorities. Frederick provost marshal Yellott went to the house of Miss Clara McAleer and confiscated her velvet slippers, which featured a Rebel flag embroidered on them.[189]

Confederate memorabilia. *Library of Congress.*

Right after Lincoln's assassination was a particularly dangerous time for secessionists to express their partisanship. On April 21, 1865, Union authorities jailed Maria and Louisa Constable of West Lombard Street in Baltimore for burning a small U.S. flag. On the same day as the arrest of these women, the military picked up two persons charged as "suspicious characters," a sufficiently vague designation to fit a variety of perceived crimes. They were joined in prison by one arrested for treasonable language, another for disloyalty and a third for cheering for Jefferson Davis. A few days later in Baltimore, Samuel Peacock was incarcerated for "blaspheming the memory of President Lincoln," and John Justin was charged with "blaspheming the deceased President and ridiculing negro soldiers."[190]

Any disloyal speech, whether verbal or symbolic, was considered grounds for arrest, although often the authorities would place the offender on notice, parole him or her or require an oath of allegiance in order to be released from custody. There seemed to be no uniformity of treatment or sentencing due to the novelty of the crimes and the frequent turnover in personnel at department headquarters and the provost marshal office. In addition, the authorities had to consider the serious crowding in many of the penal institutions and forts that were overloaded with both military and political prisoners. Fort McHenry, for example, had a total of 125 *political* prisoners between May 1861 and February 17, 1862; that number climbed to 2,094 incarcerated from the beginning of 1863 to July 1865.[191]

Smuggling, communicating with the South, crossing the lines without a pass, aiding Confederate POWs and spying were all treated more seriously than speech. Mrs. Ellen Swann and Miss Alice McGill of Hagerstown were sent across the Potomac for providing information to the Confederates in the Gettysburg campaign and for harboring enemy soldiers. Four Baltimore females—Euphemia Goldsborough and three Lomax sisters—were all exiled south via Fortress Monroe and told that they would be treated as spies if they returned. Virginia Lomax, who failed to follow these orders, was incarcerated in the Old Capitol Prison. In February 1864, three men from St. Mary's County in southern Maryland were arrested for blockade running and were tried by a military commission. Mrs. William Key Howard, Mrs. Martha Dugan and Mrs. Mary Sawyer were sent from Baltimore to the Old Capitol Prison for a variety of what were considered serious offenses. Exhibiting any signs of sympathy for Confederate POWs passing through one's area was also forbidden. Teenager Catherine Cassidy was sentenced to ten day's labor for transmitting letters to enemy soldiers in West's Building Hospital. Mrs. Edward McAdam saluted Confederate POWs as

Old Capitol Prison, where a number of Maryland secessionists were lodged. *Library of Congress.*

they marched in the streets, resulting in her arrest, and authorities detained nine women who aided POWs in transit to Point Lookout Prison.[192] These cases were indicative of the strong involvement of women in Baltimore, a phenomenon that led Sir William Howard Russell to observe that "a small war is waged by the police recently appointed by Federal authorities against the women, who exhibit much ingenuity in expressing their animosity to the stars and stripes."[193]

There were many other ways that individuals risked misfortune for their actions in the war. Miss Mitchell was captured at Harpers Ferry and charged as a spy after she told military authorities that she served for two years in Company A of the Eighteenth Virginia Cavalry. She was sentenced to a term in the Old Capitol Prison. It should be noted that Union authorities were clearly at a loss about what to do with a number of females who appeared in Maryland in the blue or gray uniform. Most were jailed, but one was arrested as a vagrant. Men were detained if they resisted enrollment or the draft for political or other reasons, or if they recruited for the Confederate forces. In October 1864, seven wholesale and retail businesses in Baltimore were ordered to close, and their employees were arrested on suspicion of dealing with blockade runners. Sent to the nation's capital and incarcerated, most were released and allowed to reopen the following month. A very unusual case involved the Reverend Fred Gibson of an Episcopal church on York Road, who refused to admit a boy with unionist sympathies into his school. He was arrested but released with conditions attached.[194]

The Union military was determined to send a strong message to any civilians who contemplated aiding the Confederates. Citizens living near Frederick must have been shocked and appalled by the public execution of William Richardson, a paper and map peddler who frequented the Union camps. He was found guilty of spying by a drumhead court-martial and hanged by the Pennsylvania Cavalry on a locust tree just a mile outside of town. They left his corpse on display by the roadside, rotting in the hot summer sun for a number of days. A placard was pinned to his breast that read: "Tried, convicted, and hung as a spy. Anyone cutting down the body, without orders, will take his place."[195] Federal soldier J.D. Chadwick wrote to his father on July 15, 1863, that Richardson's sentence was carried out on Monday morning at daylight, "and I saw him *still hanging on Thursday!* It was the most horrible sight I have seen. He had not a stitch of clothes on except a piece of shirt—no cap either." This event was so stunning and bizarre to the soldiers that quite a number of them mentioned this in letters.[196] For those civilians who were not battle-hardened veterans, this sight was an unforgettable and vivid warning of the dire consequences of receiving a verdict of treason. A committee of nearby residents called on Major General John Buford, demanding an explanation of this act, but they went back to their homes disgruntled with his response.[197]

Union threats to life, liberty and property extended into censorship of publications. In 1863, two editors of newspapers, one from Chestertown and one from Leonardtown, were sent south for treasonous articles. In a similar manner, the owners and publishers of the *Republican* were arrested for treason and escorted under guard to the South, and the newspaper's office was closed and locked. The *Daily Gazette*, a Baltimore publication, was taken over by the military and the editor arrested; the publishers of the *Catholic Mirror* were likewise detained at the same time. Major General Wallace, while he released Mr. Flint, the Baltimore correspondent for the *New York World*, after he had been arrested, warned Flint that his writings were offensive to the Union men of Baltimore and that he must change his style.[198] A particularly egregious case of treatment of the press involved Joseph Shaw, editor of a Democratic newspaper. When Union soldiers from the Fourth Maryland Infantry were searching for him, an informer revealed that Shaw and his staff were hiding in the cellar of their office in Westminster. They were captured and put on a rail car and then taken to

The arrest of Marshal Kane of Baltimore. *Library of Congress.*

Baltimore's Eutaw House, where Shaw said they were detained "to be gazed at and insulted by Union people and government soldiers." While Shaw was released, he was later killed by an armed unionist mob in April 1865.[199] In addition to censorship of publications, merchants purveying musical scores, portraits or artifacts honoring the Confederacy also faced shutdowns and possible arrests.

Military suppression of opinions extended into interference with clergymen and church services. Major General Lew Wallace sent a communication to the Reverend L. Van Bokkelen of St. Timothy's Church in Catonsville condemning the fact that the secessionists appeared to be forcing him into an early retirement. Wallace noted that if the reverend indeed retired, no church services would be permitted there unless the replacement was a proven loyalist.[200] This intrusion into religious affairs continued under Wallace and was extended to all congregations on April

19, 1865. The commander of the Middle Department warned the clergy that some of their members in Baltimore were failing to keep politics out of their churches and that the conduct of some of them was "positively offensive to the loyal people, and of doubtful propriety." He further noted that if they failed to follow his advice voluntarily, he had the power to enforce his commands. If they felt they could not comply, Major General Wallace counseled the clergymen to close their doors at least for the season.[201]

Federal soldiers, government detectives and unionist neighbors were all sources of intelligence on the subversive activities of the secessionists. The partisanship of the war created a class of informers that betrayed friends and neighbors to the authorities out of a variety of motives, including patriotism, envy, revenge or simply eagerness to spread gossip that they had heard. The result was that so many people in Baltimore were being accused of treason by August 1862 that Major General John Wool decided that from that point on, charges were to be submitted in writing with specifications regarding date, time and actions and that the charges must be attested to under oath.[202] When the provost marshal issued an order to this effect a few weeks later, he noted that there were too many frivolous accusations lodged on the basis of mere suspicion or rumor. The lack of credibility of some of the informants did not stop the Federals from continuing to urge that citizens report any suspicious activities. Indeed, Major General Lew Wallace issued a circular for his department on April 25, 1865, requesting that loyal citizens, while exercising moderation, should report to the provost marshal's office or to the police "such information of the whereabouts of obnoxious persons as they may at any time chance to obtain."[203] The circular related to paroled and returning Confederate officers and enlisted men and to Southern-sympathizing citizens.

Marylanders who supported the South found that there were no sanctuaries where they could escape from the heavy hand of the Union. On August 4, 1863, soldiers descended on the funeral for Confederate captain William D. Brown at Greenmount Cemetery in Baltimore. There, they arrested eighteen persons, including the father of the deceased and the undertaker, who was accused of putting a new Confederate uniform on the dead soldier. The undertaker explained that he replaced only a piece of the uniform because it was moldy. This sobering and intrusive episode was a demonstration that secessionists had no privacy, even to mourn. Those who supported the South found that the guarantees afforded by the First Amendment did not apply to them and that the Fourth Amendment's requirement of a warrant had been deferred indefinitely. When arrested, their rights as those accused of crimes were often not honored, and there were times when civilians were tried by military commissions. People were arrested for defaming Lincoln, hissing at the flag, singing "Maryland, My Maryland" and even for drawing silly caricatures of the president.[204] Some secessionists reacted to these new realities with defiance and anger, while others lived in mortal fear that the men in blue uniforms would arrive at their doors with the intention of unearthing and punishing treason.

To the secessionist activists, the Union soldiers were the local and highly visible embodiment of the tyrannical regime in the nation's capital, bent on enslaving Southerners, depriving them of their liberties and threatening their way of life. Elizabeth Howard, a wealthy and influential Baltimore matron, wrote to her husband, Charles, about the soldiers who took him and, later, her son to prison. As she recalled, these "men surrounded our house in the dead stillness of midnight and stole you away…and the gleam of those bayonets I shall never forget." As Baltimore's police commissioner, Charles Howard was one of the early targets of Union efforts to arrest Maryland's most influential political figures in a war where some citizens were considered subversives. In another letter to her husband imprisoned at Fort Warren, Elizabeth expressed her sense that the enemy occupiers in Baltimore were jailers, depriving civilians of both their physical and their intellectual freedom.

> *Dearly as I would love to see you all at home again, as matters are now, there would be no enjoyment—you would have no privileges—no, not as many as you have there. Your bodies are confined there—here both mind and body would be. You can speak your thoughts there—here you cannot.*[205]

Mrs. Howard did a great deal of socializing but was always careful to avoid political topics in public lest she, too, be incarcerated.

The heavily regimented way of life that was the byproduct of the Union occupation was a matter of both exasperation and anger. Dr. Joshua Webster Hering, living in Westminster in the summer of 1863, found the presence of the Union soldiers a great annoyance. As a doctor who did rounds, he had to pass through the Federal pickets at the edge of town. He commented that no one was permitted to leave "without first appearing before his sovereign majesty and taking the oath of allegiance to the government of the United States and getting a pass." He designated the whole process a "farce." The different treatment of people under the occupation caused a great deal of

Union soldiers search a secessionist's house for arms. *Library of Congress.*

ire and bitterness on the part of citizens who were the victims of Union pillaging or confiscation of the fruits of their labor. Dr. Hering remarked that the Southern sympathizers were never paid for their hay, horses and supplies that were taken by the soldiers.[206] It was always difficult for civilians to watch enemy soldiers benefitting from their hard work. James Francis Beall, a farmer and teacher who lived in Frederick County, was disgusted in 1862 when the Yankees came and stole his peaches, tomatoes, potatoes and melons. Of the soldiers, he said, "They are certainly the meanest set of men in the civilized world." Beall was just as incensed when Federal troops came two years later and again visited his farm. He wrote of this in his diary: "Yesterday four mean Yankees came here. They pretended to want water & went to the spring & swallowed Mollie's pot of cream sufficient to make three lbs. of butter." One week earlier, when the Confederates took two of his horses, he made no written comment on the theft, probably a reflection of his partisanship in the war.[207]

Many secessionist women, particularly in Maryland's cities and town, reacted at times with both defiance and disdain for the Union soldiers they encountered. Dr. Samuel Harrison, who lived in Baltimore for the first year of the war, witnessed a Federal officer coming out of a store wiping his face with a handkerchief after being spit on by a young lady. In another episode in the city that took place at a local store, he saw a Union soldier pass a female secessionist at the door. Harrison wrote, "She sneers and then began brushing and shaking her dress as if she had contracted some dirt from his touch—or really to express the thought she had caught *lice* from him."[208] In Frederick, a well-dressed man and woman rushed to the opposite side of the street to avoid contact with a Federal soldier and an American flag. The *Examiner*, a unionist paper, noted, "We are happy to report that this ill-bred she-rebel is not an inhabitant of Frederick and that such conduct is seldom seen here, except on the part of public women."[209] Tillie Sterling, a staunch unionist whose husband was stationed in Annapolis during the war, wrote to her mother about the "secesh loonies" in that city who were abusing Union Captain Watkins for arresting a Rebel spy. In another of Tillie's letters, she remarked that Confederate women in Annapolis, although bitter, generally behave themselves because of the presence of troops, and they "have never acted in the unladylike and outrageous manner that the women in Baltimore and other Southern cities have done."[210]

Baltimore's Southern women earned a reputation for their contemptuous attitudes toward the Union soldiers in their streets. One volunteer Zouave, witnessing firsthand the behavior of these ladies, satirized them in a leaflet that was published and distributed around the city in 1862. One stanza from the poem summarized his views on this subject:

> *Lavinia twists her coral lips awry*
> *At every red breech'd soldier passing by.*
> *Kate's glance at officers is so severe*
> *Her meaning they mistake, at times, I fear.*
> *Fanny tucks up her dress—so feeling rankles,*
> *And shows contempt, and very pretty ankles.*[211]

The Middle Department commanders, who were forced to handle the secessionist female activists, were well aware of both the single-mindedness and the remarkable success of these women in their support of the cause.

To many Confederate Marylanders, both male and female, the national government had become thoroughly despotic, imprisoning its dissidents, censoring the press and silencing any opponents. Lincoln's suspension of habeas corpus led Daniel Murray Thomas, a Baltimore resident, to conclude: "This was what cost Charles I his head, and would at this day shake Queen Victoria from her throne."[212] To those who were supportive of the South, the Union soldiers in their midst were agents of this omnipotent central government that was out of control.

7

The Union Soldier: Myth and Reality

But at length the deadly elements surged around him and swept over his household with all the suddenness of an electric storm, and with dangers vastly more dreadful to contemplate.[213]
—*Chaplain Edwin M. Haynes*

In an 1863 article in the *Herald of Freedom and Torch Light* (Hagerstown), the editors warned parents that their children were playing mock war games with stones and toy pistols. They noted: "Young America is full of the war spirit, and withal apt scholars. They have learned to form battle lines, tear down fences, throw up entrenchments, advance skirmishers, yell, curse and swear, and go through the whole programme of a real engagement."[214] It was not surprising to people living during the Civil War that children, with their vivid imaginations and zest for action and adventure, emulated their heroes in such a manner. Many young and active minds were entranced with visions of military figures on horseback or on foot, decked out in fancy uniforms, accompanied by fife and drum and carrying colorful flags. These role models were lionized in history books, cheered as they marched through the streets and accorded every accolade imaginable. The stereotype of the fearless and honorable soldier, engaged in a principled fight to the death with the enemy, was powerful and appealing to both youth and adults. But for the latter, this image, while never abandoned, became much more nuanced and complex as the war progressed. This was certainly the case in Maryland, where both armies marched and clashed in large numbers and where civilians were deeply divided on their attitudes toward soldiers on both sides of the conflict.

Both the Federal soldiers and those civilians who sustained them had a very different perspective from the secessionists regarding the purposes of the occupation of Maryland. Many Union soldiers saw themselves in the role of the "protector," pledged to safeguard the property and the liberties of the citizens from the dangers of Confederate raids or invasions. When Sergeant Robert Cruikshank, of the 123rd New York Infantry, marched through the central part of the state to the enthusiastic cheers of the residents, he believed that "all are waving us on to protect those rights that are being trampled under foot."[215] William Byrnes of the 1st Michigan Infantry, writing from Bladensburg in the first year of the war, made it clear that huge armies leave traces on the landscape, "but one thing is plain to be seen, the troops stationed in this region preserve inviolable the rights of citizens."[216] Later in the war, John Frederick Roser of the 110th Ohio Volunteer Infantry in a letter to his wife, explained: "Well, here we are in Frederic[k] County, Md. came up to protect the loyal citizens of the State from the raids of these cussed Rebels."[217] E.L. Cowart, first lieutenant of the 14th New Jersey, wrote a letter about a month after the Battle of Monocacy and expressed his wish that his regiment would have some success against the Confederates. "I hope," he said, "we shall be able to protect Maryland, for she has come out nobly for the union and the rebbies want to chastise her for this sensible act."[218] These sentiments penned by the Federal soldiers were widely affirmed in many letters and diaries of both enlisted men and their officers. The loyal citizens anticipated both safety and security from the occupiers. However, as the war progressed, soldiers and civilians lowered their expectations regarding the efficacy and value of the Union presence. This was due to both the crimes and depredations of the Federal troops and to their inability to defend state residents from the Confederates.

Marylanders on both sides of the conflict were subject to harassment, kidnapping, depredations and physical danger from Confederates over the border. John Mosby's Rangers regularly crossed the Potomac River from Virginia into southern Maryland to damage the C&O Canal and the B&O Railroad and to raid farms and stores for supplies. Those in western Maryland on the southern border had to contend with McNeill's Rangers, whose objectives were much the same as Mosby's partisans. In February 1865, Jesse McNeill and some of his men actually succeeded in making a daring raid into the city of Cumberland, then occupied by thousands of Federal troops, where in the middle of the night they kidnapped two Union generals and transported them back to Virginia. Confederate raiders passing through Urbana abducted Thomas A. Smith, a unionist storeowner, and his clerk, Frank Harris.[219] Alfred Brengle, a Frederick lawyer and a member of the Sanitary Commission, was taken, transported south and accused of giving aid and comfort to the Federals.[220] In Washington County, Mike Zimmerman, who owned a store, learned that his father was kidnapped by the Rebels and was being held for a ransom of four mules.[221] The presence of large numbers of Union troops in all of these areas did not deter these acts that continued throughout the conflict.

The seriousness of the danger from both armies first became apparent in the Antietam campaign in the fall of 1862. Ann Schaeffer wrote in her diary that the residents of Frederick heard "drums beat at dead of night striking terror and dismay into the stout loyal hearts in her midst." Fire bells later started to ring, and she woke up to see the huge bonfire in the middle of the city, as the Federals deliberately burned hospital stores so they did not fall into the hands of the enemy. Then the Union soldiers fled, "leaving the town defenseless." Some citizens were running away, while others were hiding their valuables. When she got up the next morning, on September 6, the fire was dying down, but it left behind the horrible smell of burnt hair from the mattresses.[222] According to Lewis Steiner, after the arrival of the Confederates, "the reign of terror continued, although no personal violence was done to any citizen."[223]

After the Battle of South Mountain, the 132nd Pennsylvania Infantry marched into Boonsboro. There it found that some of the inhabitants had vacated their homes when the Confederates arrived and were now returning to discover their food, livestock and fences pillaged. Shells, probably from Union artillery, had hit some of the houses there. One man came out of his residence to report that a shell had landed on the bed, but fortunately it failed to explode.[224] Nearby communities were even more devastated after the Battle of Antietam. As the *Hagerstown Herald* reported, "We understand that the majority of the houses in Sharpsburg as well as those along the whole line of battle from thence to Keedysville exhibit marks of having been under fire." The headquarters of the Army of the Potomac, in a report on September 20, 1862, acknowledged: "Every house in Sharpsburg was struck by our shells...One child was killed. Two rebels, while cooking their supper on Tuesday, were killed by one of our shots passing through the kitchen of the house where they were."[225] Elisha Hunt Rhodes, of the 2nd Rhode Island Regiment, wrote in his dairy on September 23, 1862, "The town is all battered to pieces and is not worth much."[226] Civilians wondered how they

Middletown, near South Mountain. *Library of Congress.*

would sustain their families over the coming winter with the plundering and the damage done to storage facilities, barns, fields and fences by troops on both sides.

Occasionally, a thoughtful soldier exhibited a great measure of empathy for those citizens forced into such a close encounter with the horrors of war. Union captain George Noyes, after the battle, listened to the story of a woman from Sharpsburg who sought shelter in her cellar with her family. As he explained:

> *I can imagine few situations more trying to the nerves than to be thus pent up in gloom while that tempest howled and shrieked through the air, or came hurtling in the rooms overhead...After hearing her story, I felt that a far pleasanter position would have been the very front of the battle.*[227]

Elisha Hunt Rhodes bemoaned the Union failure to prevent the Confederates from crossing the Potomac and bringing suffering to the people of Maryland and Pennsylvania. As he noted in his diary on October 15, 1862, "If this Army cannot protect the loyal states we had better sell out and go home."[228]

At the termination of the Battle of Antietam, both soldiers and civilians shared the dreadfulness of the aftermath. Indeed, the latter were compelled to continue to live for weeks or longer in the midst of the unburied and bloated corpses of men and horses, blood-saturated rocks and soil, the contamination of streams, the putrid smell and the spread of contagious diseases. As soon as the battle ended, civilians flocked to the battlefield, determined to witness the results of what had happened in their midst. As one officer noted: "The country people flocked to the battlefield like vultures, their curiosity and inquisitiveness most astonishing; while my men were at work [burying the dead] many of them stood around, dazed and awe-stricken by the terrible evidence of the great fight."[229]

The inability of Union soldiers to mitigate the worst dimensions of war for the civilian population was reinforced the following year, in the Gettysburg campaign of late June and early July 1863. Raiders from both sides left a swath of destruction and loss as they swept through Maryland on their way to and from the small town over the Pennsylvania border. In a letter to the editor of the *Herald of Freedom and Torch Light*, an angry and frustrated local citizen complained about the inability of the Union army to defend life and property. He wrote, "In Washington County the Government has failed to furnish this protection. We have been invaded—our fences burned—our wheat crops obliterated from the face of the earth—our stock driven off —our farms and Houses pillaged."[230] In both Westminster and Frederick, a skirmish occurred between Rebel and Union cavalry in the middle of town with citizens as inadvertent observers.

Mr. Rinehart, a teacher and farmer in northwest Baltimore County, had to postpone school for a week because of the Rebel invasion. He could hear the cannonading from Pennsylvania on both July 2 and 3 and observed, "Terrible times; the neighborhood swarming with soldiers and stragglers and people fleeing from near the seat of the action." On July 4, he concluded that it was "an awful independence day" because of the hostilities that he erroneously believed would continue during the holiday. To Rinehart and others, "The most exciting fearful times I ever saw have been during the invasion of Maryland and Pennsylvania, but it is all over now."[231]

In Baltimore, on June 29, 1863, the headquarters of the Eighth Army Corps issued a warning that "there is evidence that we are about to be attacked." Fear spread across the city like wildfire. "Neighbors aroused neighbors; the startling ominous clang of heavy bells shook the church-steeples and vibrated in the midnight air; three rockets from [Forts] McHenry, three from Marshall, three from Federal Hill, shot into the dark sky."[232] On July 1, 1863,

Citizens flee Sharpsburg before battle. *Library of Congress.*

Major General Schenck declared martial law, giving him unlimited power over the civil authorities. The latter were urged to continue their duties, "only in no way interfering with the exercise of the predominant power assumed and asserted by the military authority." Citizens were urged to assist in the defense of the city, barricades were erected and curfews were imposed for businesses, residents and trains. Parties of Confederates were in the Baltimore suburbs of Reisterstown and Pikesville, and communication was cut off with western Maryland as the Rebels cut telegraph lines and destroyed railroad tracks.[233] The Battle of Gettysburg was followed by the arrival in Baltimore of large numbers of wounded from both sides and Confederate POWs.

The fear, rumors and disillusionment with the Union's ability to shield the citizenry continued into the following year with the third major invasion by the Confederates, this time in the summer of 1864. As word was received

of this incursion, African Americans and some prominent loyalist families left their homes and became refugees in an effort to get safely behind Union lines. Those who remained were left to their own devices. Some soldiers were very conscious about their inability to safeguard the unionist citizens in the area. First Lieutenant Abiel Teple La Forge, of the 106th New York Volunteer Infantry, wrote in his diary about his consternation resulting from having to withdraw from Frederick as the Rebels came, leaving the loyalists defenseless. He penned, "What must have been their feelings last night when to save ourselves from capture we had to abandon the city, which was soon occupied by the enemy. I grieve at their disappointment."[234] On that same morning of July 9, 1864, Union officers Colonel William Truex, Lieutenant Colonel Caldwell Hall and Major Peter Vredenburgh were guests at the Thomas farm located a few miles south of Frederick. Vrendenburgh, of the 14th New Jersey Regiment, had become a close friend of Mr. Thomas

Battle of Antietam, 1862. *Library of Congress.*

when his unit was garrisoned nearby. As far as the family was concerned, "it was clear that they wished to retain friendly relations with Union officers who, as their guests, extended protection over the house."[235] Unbeknownst to the Thomas family as they socialized with their company that morning, the upper floor of their residence would be used later that day by Union sharpshooters aiming at the Confederates, and thus this imposing Georgian-style house became a major target for enemy artillery fire. The exigencies of war trumped all other concerns, including the friendships forged in those years and the safety and well-being of the inhabitants who happened to reside on or near the battlefield.

Private Alfred S. Roe of the Ninth New York Heavy Artillery, a participant in the Battle of Monocacy that followed the Confederate invasion across the Potomac, talked about the memories indelibly etched in his mind concerning the wheat field on the farm of the Thomas family. There, as he explained, "on that ninth of July, we had seen two harvests gathered: the one early in the morning of wheat, the staff of life, and the other at evening of men, and the reaper thereof was death."[236] There, the Army of the Valley District under Lieutenant General Jubal Early met men from the Eighth Army Corps and the Third Division, Sixth Army Corps, under the overall command of Major General Lew Wallace. The majority of the fighting occurred on the Best, Thomas and Worthington farms and around the Gambrill Mill. The citizens attempted to secure their horses by sending them up to Sugarloaf Mountain nearby, and then sought shelter in their cellars as the "battle to save Washington" raged in their yards and fields. The Thomas estate, which was located literally in the middle of the battlefield, received the most destruction. First Lieutenant John Meigs, in a letter to his mother, said, "I have rarely seen a house more scarred by battle than his...Seven shells struck the house and I counted the marks of twenty-six musket balls on *one side*."[237] The family, slaves and neighbors sheltered in the cellar heard the crash of a shell that penetrated the wall and landed in the dining room. As the battle swept back and forth across a small stream on the property, blood from the dead and wounded on both sides mingled and flowed into the water, and according to Confederate major general John B. Gordon, "when the struggle ended a crimson current ran toward the river. Nearly one half of my men and a large number of Federals fell there."[238]

In Baltimore, fifty miles to the east, residents were called on by the Union League to defend themselves against the expected arrival of the Confederates under Brigadier General Bradley T. Johnson. While Union soldiers departed

Baltimoreans barricade streets in preparation for a possible Confederate raid. *Frank Leslie's Illustrated Newspaper.*

to the outskirts of the city, thousands of citizens were given loaded muskets and full cartridge boxes. Horses, saddles, harnesses and carbines were confiscated from owners to mount and arm the civilians. Barricades were thrown up in the streets as rumors and apprehension spread throughout the population. Specie and all available funds from the banks were taken and loaded into a steamer in the harbor, and provision was made to move the state archives, if necessary. While the Rebel cavalry never penetrated beyond the outer edges of the city, the level of excitement and fear was tangible. An observant correspondent for the *New York Times* reported a "certain dignified composure from Washington City," but "from Martinsburgh, Hagerstown, and Harper's Ferry to Baltimore, and even north of that, they have spread terror…In Baltimore, especially, the exhibitions were pitiful." The *Times* pronounced this the "boldest, and probably most successful of all rebel raids." [239] The Confederates struck Montgomery County forcefully on their way to the nation's capital. As the *Sun* reported, "Since last Saturday, she has been laid in dust and desolation. Not a heart but has been saddened; not a

Confederates capture a train during an an 1864 invasion. *Frank Leslie's Illustrated Newspaper.*

home but has seen trial and affliction; not a man but has a story to tell of plunder and pillage, of robbery and ruin." [240]

The incapability of the Union troops occupying the state to safeguard Maryland's citizens and their property contributed to an elevated level of disappointment and disillusionment in the population. The degree of protection was judged as grossly inadequate for this latest invasion in particular. Even Major General Lew Wallace, commander of the Middle Department, Eighth Army Corps, recognized the important contributions

civilians made in defending Baltimore and noted, "It was thought that the regular forces were inadequate to the emergency."[241] The cumulative result was that politicians and residents were increasingly willing to resort to self-defense since Union forces were unable to perform this formidable task. Governors A.W. Bradford of Maryland and A.G. Curtain of Pennsylvania sent a joint letter to President Lincoln soon after Early's 1864 invasion in which they warned that people living in the vicinity of the Potomac River have repeatedly suffered great damage and injury: "Many of them, it is believed, as the only security against such losses in the future, are seriously considering the propriety of abandoning their present homes and seeking safety at the north." The governors asked Lincoln for permission to form a volunteer force to guard the major fords, but their request was denied.[242]

In Cumberland, in western Maryland, residents heard about the deliberate burning of Chambersburg, Pennsylvania, on July 30, 1864, and feared that the Confederates were on their way to threaten their community next. The *Alleganian* wrote, "On Monday morning the excitement increased to such a degree that business was almost universally suspended, the business houses closed, and the merchants in many instances packed and removed their goods." When word was received of the arrival of the Rebels in their area on the first of August, Brigadier General Benjamin Kelley gathered his troops about two and a half miles outside the city, while three citizen volunteer companies rapidly organized to guard Cumberland and do picket duty. In the subsequent half-day Battle of Folck's Mill, Union forces surprised and then repelled their enemy with between only forty to sixty casualties total for both sides. This was a clear case when the presence of the Federals averted damage to the town and its inhabitants. The residents of Cumberland gathered in mass to draw up resolutions thanking Kelley and his troops for their successful resistance and for saving them from the same "hordes" that had burned Chambersburg. The Confederate brigades stole many horses and cattle in the county, and they also damaged the telegraph, railroad and the C&O Canal, tempting targets for the raiders.[243] Because of its location, Cumberland experienced frequent disruptions in its communication and transportation networks, a situation affecting both the local economy and the psychological well-being of the civilians.

Defending Maryland's citizens also became an issue on the B&O Railroad and led to a debate regarding whether protection was the job of Mr. John Garrett's railroad or of Federal troops. The B&O was considered a legitimate and prized target by the Confederates throughout the war and was frequently subject to disruption, theft and vandalism. On March 30, 1865, a guerrilla band attacked one of the trains about ten miles outside Cumberland, stole money and valuables from the passengers and succeeded in capturing the U.S. mail on board.[244] In another raiding episode, citizens took matters into their own hands in the so-called Battle of Ricketts Run on October 7, 1864. A party of eleven Confederate marauders plundered the store of Alban Gilpin Thomas at night, using force and capturing the owner and his nephew in the process. Although both were released, the Rebels escaped with the goods. The neighborhood people, almost all peace-loving

Quakers, formed a posse of seventeen armed with pistols and proceeded to follow the robbers to a forested site near Rockville. There a skirmish occurred, shots were fired and Captain Bowie, one of Mosby's men, was killed. The makeshift vigilantes also managed to capture Bowie's brother in the process.[245]

Through the eyes of most Maryland civilians, the capacity of the Union army to provide protection from the depredations of the Confederates and the consequences of combat was limited; however, the alternative—a Confederate occupation of the state—was unthinkable, except perhaps by some avid secessionists. While well-read and informed residents had some knowledge of the devastation caused by Union forces in Virginia, particularly in the Shenandoah Valley, they were also aware that in 1864, the Rebels had held three Maryland towns for ransom and burned Chambersburg, just over the Mason-Dixon line.

8

Through the Union Soldiers' Eyes

A projectile came along with its deafening death-cry, and took him right in the groin, severing his limbs completely from his body…Oh, God! May I never be doomed to witness such a sight again![246]
—*C.F. Johnson*

The Union's inability to safeguard the civilian population was frustrating to both the state's residents and to many soldiers. There was no doubt that most soldiers cared deeply about the sentiments of the citizens in the areas where they camped, marched or fought. One of the first questions that these men had when they arrived in the state related to the degree of loyalty in the population. The majority of the soldiers acknowledged that they were in a predominately unionist state, particularly in western Maryland, but that there were pockets of passionate secessionists everywhere. Warren H. Freeman, of the Thirteenth Massachusetts Regiment, writing a letter to his father in 1862, was ambivalent on the issue of partisanship: "To the question about the loyalty of the people about here, they seem to be for the Union while we are here, but secession when we are away." Captain George Noyes, of the U.S. Volunteers, after mentioning the "perfect ovation" they received as they marched into Frederick, acknowledged that not all residents were out in the streets waving flags and handkerchiefs and cheering them enthusiastically. As he said, "I understood, however, that the wealthy slaveholders did not in general join in this loyal demonstration, nor could it be expected."[247] A refined ability to tell friend from foe was an

Three women show support for troops with an American flag behind them. *Library of Congress.*

Hessian barracks in Frederick, used as a hospital after the Battle of Antietam. *Photo by Acroterion.*

important asset in a state with divided loyalties, particularly if you were separated from the rest of your regiment and dependent on the goodwill of the civilian population.

Large numbers of the Federals, in their diaries and letters, discussed how strong loyalist support lifted their spirits, buttressed their morale and improved their performance. Sergeant Robert Cruikshank, of the 123rd New York Infantry, writing to his wife from Pleasant Valley, said, "There is one thing that cheers a soldier when marching through a free country and that is the waving of handkerchiefs and the cheering from the lowest hut to the largest mansion; from the two-year-old to the old and gray-headed." Albinus R. Fell, of the 6th Ohio Infantry, who was in Frederick after the Battle of Gettysburg, noted the following: "Our men fight more like devils than men—the encouragement and kind usage our soldiers receive by the people of Maryland and Pennsylvania cheers them on to victory or death."[248] Captain Noyes, in a march from the nation's capital through Maryland in 1862, noted, "There was not the roughest soldier in the ranks who did not march better, ay, and fight better, for these and other sympathetic demonstrations in Maryland." William Cline in his diary remarked that the Union sympathizers in Middletown affectionately called their troops "Blue Birdies."[249]

Union men often articulated their appreciation to the civilians who were their benefactors during the Civil War. Sergeant Henry W.T. Tisdale, of the 35th Massachusetts Infantry, wounded in the Battle of South Mountain and taken eventually to Frederick to convalesce, mentioned in his diary that the citizens came to the Lutheran Church twice a day with food, drink, reading materials and luxuries for their comfort.[250] Daniel Long, of the 151st New York Regiment, in a letter on July 18, 1864, commented on how the sidewalks in Frederick were filled with women bringing baskets filled with choice edibles to the men in the morning and then before supper.[251] Soldiers were very generous in expressing their gratitude to the nurses in the makeshift field hospitals and the U.S. general hospitals in the state, to the Union Relief Associations found in every city and town and to the many supporters who welcomed them in their homes. In some cases, particularly when they spent a lot of time in proximity to the civilians, soldiers saw their benefactors as a substitute family. Nathan Parameter, from the 29th Ohio Regiment, while in the hospital in Frederick, "found a 'Mother' in the person of Mrs. Cooper Smith and a 'Sister' in the person of a very pretty young lady from Ohio."[252]

Federal soldiers near populated areas routinely relied on civilians to provide refreshments such as water and lemonade or for something to supplement their rations. There were times when government supply wagons were unable to keep pace with soldiers on the march, leaving the men to fend for themselves. W.A. Roberts, of the 45th Pennsylvania Regiment, told his parents in a letter: "The Government also allows each man forty cents a day for rations, over half the time we are situated so that we cannot get the rations and consequently have to forage and sometimes pay double for what we purchase, provided we cannot confiscate it."[253] Under these circumstances, civilians often provided handouts of food and drink in the streets or even hospitality and victuals in their homes. Famished soldiers from the 118th Pennsylvania Volunteers passing through Frederick were on the quest for a meal when they saw a curious woman in Quaker clothing peering out her window. One enterprising man greeted her, dipped his cap politely and inquired: "Madam, what is there in the village?" The woman replied, "A college of some reputation, sir." He testily answered, "Good heavens, madam, I can't eat a college" and marched onward.[254]

Some Union soldiers who came from out of state were bewildered by the diversity that they found in Maryland. Samuel McClain, of the 144th Ohio National Guard, stationed at Camp Parole in Annapolis in 1864, was struck by the differences between home and his post. When he went to church, he observed three women in the congregation while the rest were soldiers. He wrote, "Here all men and no women, thare [sic] all women and no men…This state is composed of Negroes, dogs & fools & Rebs. The women are all so fetched homely."[255] Daniel Preston Adams, whose job was to guard the hospitals on Camden Street, was disoriented and confused by the size of Baltimore and diversity of its culture. In a letter to his sister, he wrote about the people of all colors and the horses and drays moving in every direction. He called the city a wilderness because he could travel all day and never get out of it.[256] A small number of wounded, miserable and disgruntled soldiers found nothing pleasant about either the state or its people. Solon Rand, a patient in Patterson Park Hospital in Baltimore, wrote to his uncle that the doctors were drunk, they were selling the rations that should go to the men and the sick were treated worse than dogs. Regarding the city, he found it "a miserable dirty rebel hole and they cannot whitewash it over."[257]

Union soldiers perceived the Confederate supporters as potential enemies and at times accused them of spying and informing for the enemy. John Hoffman, of the Ninety-fifth Pennsylvania Infantry, blamed the Copperheads for the Union defeat at Monocacy Junction in 1864, accusing them of informing the Rebels about Federal movements.[258] First Lieutenant E.Y. Goldsborough, aide de camp to Brigadier General

A woman helps a Union soldier write home. *Library of Congress.*

Erastus B. Tyler, said much the same. He wrote, "From their friends in Frederick [the rebel sympathizers] they had obtained information on our movements and strength."[259] Union soldiers resented any such assistance, which they perceived as a treasonous betrayal. William Kirkwood, of the First Maryland Regiment, believed that the Copperheads were prolonging the war and that the "traitors at home" were worse than the Confederate army:

> *I despise them more than I do the Rattlesnakes who are in arms and brave enough to fight on our front. I honor them more than I do the cowardly traitor in my rear who are doing all they can to annoy the union citizens and enjoying all the comforts of a prosperous country, which they are trying to destroy while we are suffering the passions and hardships of war.*[260]

The presence of this activist Southern-sympathizing minority prevented the Union soldiers and authorities from feeling entirely at ease among civilians.

It is ironic that while Union men complained bitterly about secessionist civilians providing information on their numbers and movements to the Confederates, the Federals followed the same practice in Maryland. First Lieutenant Charles Kirk acknowledged that while they were in Hagerstown, the unionists kept them posted on the locations of the Rebels and in other ways provided them with valuable intelligence.[261] A citizen of Baltimore who was in Frederick as the Confederates briefly occupied it in 1862 passed on information regarding this to Major General Wool. Other civilians communicated with Union authorities about Major General J.E.B. Stuart's cavalry movements around the Union army in October 1862.[262] These were common and often fruitful routines that both sides employed to supplement what they gathered from their own scouts and spies.

Union soldiers did feel more comfortable in some parts of the state than others. Federal troops in their journals, letters and regimental histories expressed great affection for towns like Boonsboro, Middletown and Frederick for the startling beauty of their surrounding landscape and for the undying loyalty, patriotism and devotion of their citizens. So many of the troops mentioned the overwhelmingly enthusiastic and welcoming reception that they received each time they were in Frederick. And yet, even there, the secessionists retained their defiance and their activities to aid their cause. In the aftermath of the Antietam campaign, the jail in Frederick was filled with about five hundred Confederate POWs, and Colonel Allen, the military governor there, was confronted with a very difficult situation. Friends of the prisoners tried to break them out of jail by setting it on fire, hoping that the Confederates could escape in the chaos. Swift action from firefighters prevented that from occurring. At the same time, Allen's office "was besieged with rebel women, hours at a time, with unblushing effrontery, for permission to go and see and cheer, or take these articles into the jail and give to the dear, suffering boys." A clerk in the office mentioned that usually two came in at once ("they hunt in pairs") to beg and plead their cause, exhibiting an unmatched persistency. They brought gray clothing with them, arguing that it was the cheapest color of fabric and that they were not trying to show their patriotism to the enemy.[263] The Union men reacted with both amusement and indignation to the women who refused to take "no" for an answer.

Soldiers camped along the Potomac, guarding the river, C&O Canal and B&O Railroad, were on the watch not just for the Rebels across the water but also for smugglers and spies in the civilian population. Henry Blake, a Union soldier stationed near Bladensburg and Budd's Ferry, found the secessionists polite and hospitable while simultaneously carrying out their illegal and treasonous schemes. He mentioned an incident where a Federal officer, a frequent guest of an upper-class family living nearby, got engaged to their lovely daughter. She manipulated him into using his influence to secure the release of her brother from prison in Fort Lafayette. As soon as her brother was freed and safe, she broke the engagement and treated him with nothing but scorn and contempt.[264]

The greatest suspicion among Union soldiers was reserved for the residents of Baltimore, primarily as a result of the Pratt Street Riot in April 1861. Willard Glazier, of the Second Regiment New York Cavalry, recalled the poet's prophecy as they rode through the city a few months after the riot:

> *And the eagle, never dying, still is trying, still is trying,*
> *With its wings upon the map to hide a city with its gore;*
> *But, the name is there forever, it shall be hidden never,*
> *While the awful brand of murder points the Avenger to its shore;*
> *While the blood of peaceful brothers God's dread vengeance doth implore,*
> *Thou art doomed, O Baltimore.*[265]

The threats of retaliation against the Southern sympathizers and the misgivings about the loyalties of the residents diminished with time but never entirely disappeared during the war.

Potomac River and C&O Canal. Confederate raiders regularly crossed the river to damage the C&O Canal and the B&O Railroad. *Detroit Publishing Company Collection, Library of Congress.*

The Twenty-first Massachusetts Volunteers marched through the city on August 25, 1861, with fixed bayonets and loaded weapons, when their colonel told them they were in the "enemy's country" and had to be on full alert. The men of the "Ulster Guard" (Twentieth New York State Militia) were told not to advance through the center of Baltimore to reach Camp Patterson Park because of potential trouble. While Theodore Gates of that unit found many warm and welcoming unionists in the city, he noted that the "young bloods" were persistent secessionists. As he observed: "The tone of 'society' was decidedly disloyal, and Jeff Davis could hardly have had more enthusiastic and persuasive emissaries than were to be found among the beautiful women of the Monumental City."[266] The colonel of the Thirty-seventh Pennsylvania Infantry ordered his men as they passed through Baltimore to do so "in a quiet and respectful manner. Offer no insults—disturb no one. You have all your pieces loaded, and if we are assaulted, defend yourself." Soon after they arrived, a rumor was rapidly spreading through the camp that one soldier was dead and another very ill because the lemonade they purchased was poisoned by a secessionist.

The need to "beware of the enemies in your midst" led some Union soldiers to both resent the Southern sympathizers and even, in certain cases, to strike back against them. Charles Lynch, of the Eighteenth Connecticut Infantry, stationed at Fort McHenry in September 1862, witnessed Confederate prisoners of war incarcerated briefly at that location pending exchanges. There, he wrote, secessionist women arrived with food and encouragement for the POWs, neglecting the wounded Union soldiers nearby. "No notice was taken of them. That was more than the Connecticut boys could stand. A raid was made on the Baltimoreans, they were run out of the fort, the supplies confiscated and given to the disabled Union soldiers who were in need of some comforts."[267] Reaction against the secessionists by Union soldiers took a variety of forms, including vandalism and pillaging their property, turning them in to the authorities and unauthorized searches and seizures.

The bluecoats had more to worry about than just the enemy and the secessionist supporters. Three residents of Port Tobacco shot at men from the 13th New Hampshire Regiment for no apparent reason, while in Annapolis, in March 1864, four soldiers were found murdered with their throats cut.[268] Punishment from military authorities for misconduct was at times arbitrary and severe. Brigadier General Willoughby in Baltimore bemoaned the uncivilized and savage methods used against those who misbehave: "Men can be seen here in stocks daily, wearing and working with ball and chain, 'bucked and gagged,' and even knocked down by the fist or the club of the Provost Marshal."[269] Such practices were widespread. In addition, soldiers had to endure the privations of the incessant marching that characterized major campaigns, often in the heat of the summer, resulting in sunstroke for some. The men of the 114th New York Regiment were disgusted and complaining about marching "hither and thither, in pursuit of the enemy, never able to find him. It seemed a useless labor to pass between Monocacy and Harpers Ferry, three times in a single week."[270] Stephen Minot Wells, from the headquarters of the First Army Corps at Berlin, Maryland, wrote about the pursuit of General Lee after Gettysburg: "We are wanderers on the face of the earth, like the Israelites of old. We don't stop twenty-four hours in the same place, but keep up this eternal marching all the time."[271]

Soldiers were struck with unimaginable war weariness. Josiah Lewis Hall, of the 110th Ohio Regiment, wrote in his diary on July 19, 1864, "Oh when will the civil war have an end[?] I wish I could see the end[.] O what shall the future be[?] When shall the Great God arise in his might and stop this cruel war[?]"[272] Some of the soldiers simply could not handle the grief and the trauma. John Jacques described a tragic and deplorable

A Union soldier with his family. *Library of Congress.*

incident that occurred involving one of their men as they camped near the Monocacy River. A soldier from Company B "loaded a musket, and placing it under his chin, pulled the trigger with his foot, and launched his soul into eternity."[273] In another horrible event, substitute William Briscoe, who was stationed at Camp Hicks on the Eastern Shore, was "suddenly afflicted with a fit of madness and destroyed his clothing and tore his flesh from his limbs."[274]

This context in which the soldier operated helped to explain some of the reasons behind the lack of discipline, the prevalence of alcohol abuse and the crimes against the persons and the property of noncombatants. There were numerous causes operating simultaneously and reinforcing one another. Incorporated in every army were evil and unscrupulous men, driven by greed, revenge, ambition or envy. The prevalence of alcohol, despite the military's attempt to control it, lowered inhibitions and raised the aggression levels of many of the individuals under the influence. The concern with one's peer group—whether it was the regiment, the company or just a subset of such a unit—led soldiers to commit acts in conjunction with others that they might not have done individually. The authority conferred by their uniform and weapons facilitated their ability to dominate and victimize the citizens residing in their midst. The transient nature of the soldier that effectively undermined ties with the community made accountability for actions more problematic and contributed to a general feeling of upheaval.

But the explanation for the persistent and unacceptable level of troublesome and illegal behavior was more complicated than the factors mentioned thus far. Men who fought in war became fundamentally different people during and after their experience with combat. The stress, anguish and horror of battle transformed the Civil War soldier in a manner that was not fully comprehended at that time. One of the sharpshooters who spent the entire night after the Battle of Antietam expressed his torment very clearly:

> *The sights were terrifying; sounds horrible and startling. A kind of hardness crept over us during the long, wakeful night we passed in that blood-stained, death strewn spot by the Burnside Bridge, and we grew older in thought and feeling by having come in contact with such misery and suffering, which we nearly so fully realized afterwards.*[275]

Decades after the battles, men wrote in very graphic and stark language about the scenes on the battlefield as if it were yesterday. C.F. Johnson, of the Eighth New York Infantry, talked about the piles of Rebel dead along the roadside as they marched over the west side of South Mountain, commenting on their "ghastly faces and beamless eyes," but one Rebel in particular captured his attention. "I noticed one man, a large powerfully built soldier, with a huge beard and moustache, and why it is I cannot tell, but he haunts my memory above all the rest."[276] These men knew that even victories were purchased at perhaps too high cost as they witnessed the bloodbath, saw the mangled, bloated and blackened bodies of their friends and tried to come to terms with their own mortality. Assuming responsibility for the killing of a fellow human being was a task that no sensitive and thoughtful person could fully come to terms with, particularly those with strong religious or moral convictions. Sergeant Walter S. Goss, like many of his fellow soldiers, questioned the sanity of it all. "Blue and gray lay stretched in the cold grasp of death: and yet the carnage must go on, though mothers weep and widows moan: though homes are desolated, what care we? We are making history with thundering noise, writing it in the letters of blood."[277]

The immediate and long-range effects of combat on soldiers were poorly comprehended in the nineteenth century and remain only partially explicable today. Recent advances in knowledge in the fields of medicine and psychiatry, supported by studies of veterans of Vietnam, the Gulf War and the conflicts in Afghanistan and Iraq, have enlarged our understanding of war-induced physical and mental illnesses that resulted from exposure to combat, to dead and decaying bodies and to losses of comrades. Those

A soldier next to makeshift graves at Burnside's Bridge. *Library of Congress.*

trained to kill who witnessed violence on a mass scale were more likely to develop such anti-social tendencies as substance abuse, lower flash points for violence and a higher incidence of mental disorders. All of these environmental factors contributed to a higher prevalence of crime, depredations and disorderly conduct among soldiers that was manifested in Maryland and elsewhere from 1861 to 1865. When life is so fragile, as it is in war, other values—sociability, order, discipline and responsibility—were subject to challenges not present during times of peace.

A study done by University of California (Irvine) researchers in 2008 provides concrete evidence that Civil War soldiers were prone to the same psychiatric scars—anxiety, depression, PTSD, alcohol abuse, etc.—that afflict those in more modern conflicts. The researchers matched the military records of 17,700 veterans to postwar medical records of the U.S. Pension Board surgeons. According to the study published in the *Archives of General Psychiatry*: "We found strong relations between traumatic exposure (e.g. witnessing a larger percentage of company death), co-morbid disease, mental health ailments, and early death." In the pension records there were references to "soldier's heart," "exhausted heart" or "nostalgia," vague terms yet still expressive of the reality that war can be profoundly damaging to the human psyche.[278]

No matter how hard they tried, citizens who had never been in combat experienced difficulty understanding the mindset of the Civil War soldier. Harry Kiefer, a drummer boy with the 150th Pennsylvania Regiment, mentioned in his recollections a scene that occurred as his unit marched back from the Battle of Gettysburg through Maryland. They were remarkably quiet, many of them remembering comrades who were not returning with them. They came upon a group of young ladies and gentlemen who were jubilant and elated at the Union victory, so they cheered and sang for the soldiers. Kiefer said they tried to give the civilians three cheers in return, but they were too heavy-hearted. "Somehow after the first hurrah, the other two stuck in our throats and died away soundless on the air. And so we only said, "God bless you, young friends, but we can't cheer today, you see!"[279] Many of the soldiers did not fully understand the reasons for the psychological crash that often occurred after battle, even when their side prevailed over the enemy. Colonel Frederick Hitchcock, who remained on the field in Sharpsburg for several days after the Battle of Antietam, said that he, Colonel Wilcox and Major Shreve were all so miserable "as to be scarcely able to remain on duty." He attributed the despondency to poor meals and "the nervous strain through which we had passed." The soldiers of the 35th Massachusetts Volunteers also witnessed the sight of their own dead at Antietam, "and the grave fact that we had engaged to be, and had become, slayers of our fellowmen stared us in the face, without the glamor of flash oratory and colored lights about it."[280]

Many soldiers in the Civil War went off to the front accompanied by the accolades, waving flags and parades that generated excitement and a feeling of empowerment and importance. They were the representatives of their community, fueled by the elixir of patriotism and buttressed by the belief that "God was on our side." Reality arrived very quickly with the initial harshness and regimentation of camp life, the disappointments of defeat in battle and the confrontations with civilians who did not support their side in the conflict. While the military authorities and the overwhelming unionist media supported and perpetuated stereotypes that their enemies were robbers, barbarians, vandals and cruel slaveholders, the reality was that both sides had their plunderers and criminals, and in Maryland and other border states, some supporters of both the Union and Confederate cause were slaveholders at the onset of the war. Soldiers, just like civilians, exhibited the extraordinary patriotism, fortitude and courage needed to persevere, but they were also susceptible to all the pitfalls and evils accompanying the conduct of war.

Legacy: The Quest for Normalcy

F rederick Wild, a Union veteran and regimental historian, was recalling two brothers he knew, one from the Confederate Baltimore Battery of Light Artillery and the other from its Union counterpart. These two soldiers would meet on opposite sides of the field in the Battle of Winchester, one of the many reasons why Wild called civil wars "the meanest of all wars."[281] In Maryland, the partisanship that sometimes destroyed friendships and fractured families made the task of reconciliation all the more difficult. Abraham Lincoln, in his second inaugural address, recognized that Americans would need to "bind up the nation's wounds, to care for him who shall have borne the battle, and for his widow and his orphan." The return to normalcy that citizens and veterans so desired was not easily achieved because the wounds were multifaceted—physical, psychological and sectional. Time was essential to dissipate the poisonous atmosphere and to reduce the bitterness left behind by defeat, death of loved ones or disappointment in the outcome, which for some went too far and for others not far enough. The deep and abiding interest in our Civil War long after its termination was due both to its uniqueness and to its incorporation of themes that are universal to human conflict.

In a number of modern wars, such as the civil war in Syria, civilians have been deliberately and maliciously targeted as an official policy. That was not the case in the U.S. Civil War, although there were exceptions. Treasonous activities carried the possibility of the death penalty, and there were civilians executed. A small number of individual soldiers were responsible for citizen

A Confederate woman in mourning dress with a child. *Library of Congress.*

casualties in cases involving criminal activity or negligence, as has been documented here. The increasing destructive power of the weaponry in the Civil War also resulted in wounding or killing civilians, but such instances were rare in Maryland. State residents who did suffer from military activity here were generally victimized by assault, property destruction, business losses, theft and vandalism. Those who held slaves were forced by the dynamics of war to forfeit their ownership of those living in bondage. Civilians were inconvenienced, stressed and even terrorized, the latter particularly the case for those residing in combat zones such as Sharpsburg, South Mountain and Monocacy Junction.

It should be noted that states in the Confederacy experienced an undetermined but much higher civilian death count than Maryland due to a variety of factors that disproportionately affected African American slaves. Studies completed by historians Jim Downs, James Oakes and Thavolia Glymph have demonstrated that increased black mortality resulted from overcrowded and disease-ridden contraband camps, epidemics of smallpox and cholera and violence directed against slave women and children, who were unprotected and marginalized.[282] Recent historical research has indicated that both soldier and civilian deaths in the Civil War were higher than the original postwar estimates. In a sense, the American Civil War was but a small sampling and a foreshadowing of the steady acceleration of civilian casualties that occurred in conflicts in the twentieth and twenty-first centuries.

The militarization of Maryland ended within a year of General Robert E. Lee's surrender at Appomattox. The Union army as a whole rapidly demobilized, with most men mustered out and discharged in the summer of 1865. The Army Reorganization Act of 1866 dramatically reduced the size of the army, limiting it to forty-five infantry, ten cavalry and five artillery regiments.[283] The drawing down of the military force in such a hurried manner was due to a number of factors, including America's tradition against the presence of a large standing army and the intense desires of the men to return home to their families and occupations. Both soldiers and civilians expressed revulsion at the horrors and casualties of the Civil War. In addition, the United States, still preoccupied with internal development and industrialization, had no need for large military budgets or formidable military forces.

The Army Reorganization Act of 1866 referred to above provided that four of the infantry and two of the cavalry regiments were to be reserved for African Americans, a testament to their efficacy in the late conflict.

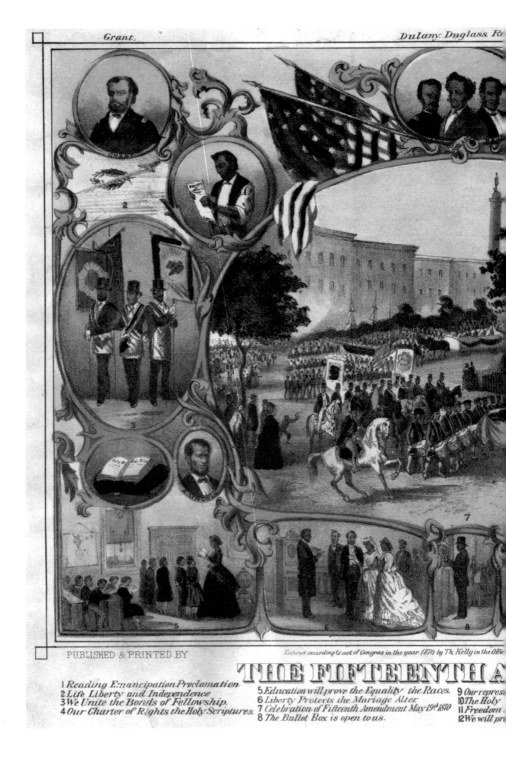

PUBLISHED & PRINTED BY

Entered according to act of Congress in the year 1871 by Th. Kelly in the Offic

THE FIFTEENTH A

1 Reading Emancipation Proclamation
2 Life Liberty and Independence
3 We Unite the Bonds of Fellowship.
4 Our Charter of Rights the Holy Scriptures.

5 Education will prove the Equality the Races.
6 Liberty Protects the Mariage Alter.
7 Celebration of Fifteenth Amendment May 19th 1870
8 The Ballot Box is open to us.

9 Our repres
10 The Holy
11 Freedom
12 We will pr

Celebration of the ratification of the Fifteenth Amendment in Baltimore. *Library of Congress.*

However, the segregation of the units was indicative of the continued racism and prejudice that afflicted much of the nation. In Maryland and elsewhere below the Mason-Dixon line, the rise of Jim Crow laws undermined the words and the spirit of the post–Civil War amendments that provided freedom, citizenship, equal protection and enfranchisement of black males. The abolitionist spirit succeeded in inducing emancipation but not social or political equality for the newly liberated men and women. Maryland-born Frederick Douglass, six years after the war, asked all Americans to consider a very important question: "If we ought to forget a war which has filled our land with widows and orphans; which has made stumps of men of the very flower of our youth, and sent them on the journey of life armless, legless, maimed and mutilated; which has…swept uncounted thousands of men into bloody graves, I say that, if this is to be forgotten, I ask, in the name of all things sacred, what shall men remember?"[284] Douglass must have been deeply disappointed when his native state refused to ratify the Fourteenth and Fifteenth Amendments to the U.S. Constitution. They failed to pass in the Maryland General Assembly until 1959 and 1973, respectively.

Segregation in the armed forces was not ended until Harry Truman's presidency, and while racism remained problematic, eligibility for participation on the basis of equality eventually broadened to include all able-bodied males and females in the appropriate age bracket. A decision was made recently to permit qualified women to serve in combat positions. In reality, women have participated in U.S. wars all the way back to the American Revolution and were certainly a presence in both the Union and the Confederate armies from 1861 to 1865. The Civil War Trust maintains that a conservative estimate of their numbers was 400 to 750. Because females were required to assume aliases, dress as men and keep their gender a secret in order to remain in the ranks, the total number of women who fought was unknown. This issue was familiar to those in the military and to the literate civilian population during the Civil War because arrests of women in uniform were catalogued in the newspapers throughout the conflict. For example, two young Maryland women, one from Hagerstown and the other from Sharpsburg, shared the adventures and perils of war with their male loved ones in Major General Pope's forces until caught at Culpepper Court House in Virginia. A young woman, who called herself Goodman," was taken into custody when she attempted to join the Purnell Legion then located near Frederick. Mary French, a seventeen-year-old from Hagerstown, remained with the Eighth West Virginia Infantry until she was arrested. She was serving with her brother, and she told the authorities that the men in Company D were well aware that she was female. A number of women in uniform were arrested at Harpers Ferry, including two with the First West Virginia Cavalry and one with the Eighty-eighth Pennsylvania Infantry.[285] These and many other illustrations demonstrated that some women were both motivated and fit for combat, but that idea was revolutionary and contrary to all gender conventions of the nineteenth century.

In addition to the expansion of the recruitment pool to encompass a much broader proportion of the population, the relationship between American civilians and soldiers has also changed dramatically in other ways since the Civil War. With the exception of the forcible removal of Native Americans to reservations and the attack on Pearl Harbor, wars since 1865 have been fought on foreign territory. Civilians continued to participate on the homefront through the draft, taxes, bonds, working in war plants and economic sacrifices, until the recent wars in the Persian Gulf, Iraq and Afghanistan. These conflicts since the end of the Cold War have not engaged the majority of the civilian population in any significant way. The draft was terminated, engagement abroad had not been financed through higher taxation and interest in the conflicts dropped sharply after the initial deployment and fighting. Families and friends of those in today's all-volunteer force remained the exceptions to this lack of connectivity between civilians and soldiers, as the burden of defense fell on a much smaller percentage of the citizenry.

Freud called warfare "the destructive instinct," and this was never clearer than in the Civil War when Americans sacrificed an estimated 620,000 to 750,000 lives. This conflict brought to the surface both "the better angels of our nature," as Lincoln expressed it, and the incarnate demons that all humans possess. Regarding Maryland civilians, there was an extraordinary level of public benevolence in the state, with citizens providing for and sustaining men of both North and South. Many residents invited soldiers into their homes, nursed them in their living rooms and in hospitals, sewed and cooked for them and even, in some cases, sacrificed their loved ones for the cause. But there were others, the enablers and the war profiteers, who found an infinite variety of ways to benefit from the weaknesses and misfortunes of the soldiers and from the resource demands of both governments.

For some of those who fought, the Civil War was an opportunity to express an elevated level of courage, honor, patriotism and gallantry. One such individual was Massachusetts soldier Oliver Wendell Holmes Jr., who was wounded at Antietam and nursed back to health at the residence of

Soldiers return home. *Harper's Weekly.*

a Hagerstown woman, Frances Howell Kennedy. Holmes, in a Memorial Day speech decades later, said of his wartime experience, "It is required of a man that he share the action and passion of his time at the peril of being judged not to have lived. Through our good fortune in our youth, our hearts were touched with fire."[286] His words were also applicable to Maryland's civilians, because so many experienced the fearful excitement of war and felt the intensity of emotion that led to involvement. The relationship between the state's citizens and the soldiers in the Civil War was testimony to blurring of the lines between homefront and battlefield, a phenomenon that has become increasingly commonplace in modern warfare. Both the military and civilians struggled with the physical devastation, the lives lost and the psychological scars that for some never healed.

Notes

ABBREVIATIONS USED:

CW—crossroadsofwar.org
MdHS—Maryland Historical Society
MSA—Maryland State Archives
LOC—Library of Congress
MON—Monocacy Archives
OR—Official Records
WB—whilbr.org

NEWSPAPER ABBREVIATIONS:

AG—*Annapolis Gazette*—(MSA)
PQ—ProQuest Historical Newspapers
BC—*Baltimore Clipper*—(MSA)
SB—*Sun* (Baltimore)—PQ
EG—*Easton Gazette*—(MSA)
VR—*Valley Register* (Middletown)—(CW)
FE—*Frederick Examiner*—(CW)
HFTL—*Herald of Freedom & Torch Light*—(CW)

Introduction

1. HFTL, June 26, 1861.
2. Department of Defense (2013 figures); Civil War Trust; Congressional Research Service.
3. Alfred S. Roe, *Fifth Regiment, Massachusetts Volunteer Militia* (Boston: Fifth Regt. Veteran Assn., 1911), 297–8.
4. Wilder Dwight, *Life and Letters of Wilder Dwight* (Boston: Ticknor & Fields, 1868), 171–2.
5. SB, March 10, 1864 (PQ).
6. Letter from Charles N. Tenney to Sister, September 26, 1862 (University of Virginia Library Online).
7. William H. Beach, *The First New York (Lincoln) Cavalry* (New York: Lincoln Cavalry Assn., 1902), 274–5.
8. *Personal Narratives of Events in the War of the Rebellion* (Providence, RI: Soldiers and Sailors Historical Society, 1885), 9–10.
9. Irvin Bell Wiley, *The Life of Billy Yank* (Baton Rouge: LSU Press, 1951), 112.
10. Scott Sumpter Sheads and Daniel Carroll Toomey, *Baltimore During the Civil War* (N.p.: Toomey Press, 1997), 64.

Chapter 1

11. Alfred Davenport, *Camp and Field Life of the Fifth New York Volunteer Infantry* (New York: Dick & Fitzgerald, 1897), 91.
12. Will H. Lowdermilk, *History of Cumberland, Maryland* (Washington, D.C.: James Anglim, 1878), 397–9.
13. Sir William Howard Russell, *My Diary North and South* (Boston: T.O.H.P. Burnham, 1863), 375 (LOC).
14. "Wartime Annapolis," *Baltimore County Advocate*, November 30, 1861 (Enoch Pratt Online).
15. SB, August 23, 1862; August 27, 1862 (PQ).
16. VR, January 10, 1862 (CW).
17. Jesse W. Dixon, *Reminiscent Essays* (circa 1924) (MON).
18. North American Forts, 1526–1956 (www.northamericanforts.com).
19. *Dear Eagle: The Civil War Correspondence of Stephen H. Bogardus, Jr.*, www.valstar.net/~jcraig/bogardus.htm.
20. Thomas Kirwin, *Memorial History of the 17th Regiment Massachusetts Volunteer Infantry* (Dorchester, MA: Henry Splaine, 1911), 105.

21. Michael Guinan Civil War Correspondence, 1862–1863, Letter to Sister, October 29, 1862 (MdHS).

22. Letter of Melville Hayward to Aunt, July 10, 1862, in Timothy J. Orr, *Last to Leave the Field* (Knoxville: University of Tennessee Press, 2011).

23. *Baltimore American & Commercial Advertiser*, May 18, 20 and 29, 1861.

24. HTFL, July 3, 1861 (CW); SB, July 12 and 9, 1861 (PQ).

25. *Baltimore Daily Gazette*, April 11, 1863 (Enoch Pratt Online).

26. Dixon, "A Boy's View of the Civil War," *Reminiscent Essays.*

27. Benjamin Diffinbaugh Diary (WB).

28. SB, July 2, 1861 (PQ).

29. S. Roger Keller, *Events of the Civil War in Washington County Maryland* (Shippensburg, PA: Burd St. Press, 1995), 357.

30. BC, July 22, 1864 (MSA).

31. Keller, *Events of the Civil War*, 45.

32. FE, December 17, 1862 (CW).

33. SB, May 15, 1861 (PQ).

34. *Baltimore American & Daily Advertiser,* May 17, 1861.

35. *South* (Baltimore), May 7, 1861 (MSA).

36. HFTL, October 15, 1862 (CW).

37. *Official Records of the Union and Confederate Armies* (hereinafter *OR*), ser. 2, vol. 1 (Washington, D.C.: Government Printing Office, 1894), 610.

38. SB, September 3, 1863 (PQ).

39. Sheads and Toomey, *Baltimore*, 84.

40. *OR*, ser. 1, vol. 33, 885.

41. SB, April 15, 1862 (PQ).

42. Letter of Samuel Hambleton and James L. Martin to James A. Pearce, May 29, 1862 (MSA).

43. Letter of George Vickers to William Price, June 3, 1862, in Abraham Lincoln Papers (LOC).

44. EG, May 9, 1863 (MSA).

45. LaFayette Baker, *Secret Service* (Washington, D.C.: National Tribune, 1894), 89.

CHAPTER 2

46. Richard T. Auchmuty, *Letters of Richard Tylden Auchmuty, Fifth Corps, Army of the Potomac* (N.p.: privately printed, n.d.), 93.

47. George F. Noyes, *The Bivouac and the Battlefield* (New York: Harper and Brothers, 1863), 330 (LOC).

48. H.H. McClune, *Camp Life* (Baltimore, MD: John D. Toy, 1862), 2, 27.

49. Rev. Theodore Gerrish, *Army Life* (Portland, ME: Hoyt, Fogg, & Donham, 1882), 45.

50. Roe, *Fifth Regiment*, 298–9.

51. *Diary of Jacob Engelbrecht* (Historical Society of Frederick County, 2001).

52. William Jordon Jr., ed., *The Civil War Journals of John Mead Gould* (Baltimore, MD: Butternut and Blue, 1997) (MON).

53. Tom Hinds, *Tales of War Times* (Watertown, NY: Herald, 1904), 19–20.

54. Mark Grimsley, *The Hard Hand of War* (New York: Cambridge University Press, 1995), 107.

55. *OR*, ser. 1, vol. 19, part 3, 335.

56. Charles Wolcott, *Twenty-First Regiment, Massachusetts Volunteers* (Boston: Houghton, Mifflin, 1882), 188.

57. *Report of Lewis H. Steiner* (Frederick, MD, 1862), 26 (Hathi Trust Digital Library).

58. Lorien Foote, *The Gentlemen and the Roughs: Violence, Honor, and Manhood in the Union Army* (New York: NYU Press, 2010), 7, 28, 67, 133.

59. Ramold, *Baring the Iron Hand*, 3, 81, 121.

60. Ibid., 105, 123, 264, 326.

61. Wiley, *Life of Billy Yank*, 248.

62. Articles of War (1806), (Illinois USGenWeb Project).

63. Lieber Code, Avalon Project (Lillian Goldman Law Library, Yale, 2008).

64. SB, July 10, 1861 (PQ).

65. George Perkins, *A Summer in Maryland and Virginia* (Chillicothe, OH: School Publishing Co., 1911), 63–4.

66. Frederick Wild, *Memoirs and History of Captain F.W. Alexander's Baltimore Battery of Light Artillery* (Baltimore: Press of Maryland School for Boys, 1912), 112, 115.

67. Alfred Davenport, *Camp and Life of the Fifth NY Volunteer Infantry* (New York: Dick and Fitzgerald, 1879), 94–96, 101–2.

68. SB, September 6, 1861; December 9 and 12, 1862; January 31, 1862 (PQ).

69. Baltimore Battery Light Artillery Records (MdHS).

70. VR, October 10, 1862 (CW).

71. Martin A. Haynes, *A Minor War History* (Lakeport, NH: private printing, 1916), 140.

72. Warren Freeman, Letter to Father, October 3, 1862 (www.soldierstudies.org).

73. Robert G. Carter, *Four Brothers in Blue* (Washington, D.C.: Gibson Brothers, 1913), 50.

74. Josh Hicks, "Contractors Face PSTD in War Zones" *Washington Post*, December 12, 2012.

75. David Wroe, "Soldiers' Mental Illness Rises Along with Tours of Duty," *Sydney Morning Herald*, August 9, 2013.

Chapter 3

76. Allen Diehl Albert, ed., *History of the 45th Regiment Pennsylvania Veteran Volunteer Infantry* (Williamsport, PA: Grit Publishing, 1912), 50.

77. FE, March 15, 1865 (CW); SB, September 3, October 2, 1863 (PQ).

78. Chauncey F. Worthington, ed., *A Cycle of Adams Letters*, vol. 2 (Boston: Houghton Mifflin, 1920), 75.

79. SB, September 5, 1863; December 13, 1861 (PQ); BC, August 2, 1864 (MSA).

80. Richard Eddy, *History of the 60th Regiment NYS Volunteers* (Philadelphia: author, 1864), 69–70.

81. SB, December 7, 1863; March 24, 1865 (PQ); BC, August 23, 1864 (MSA).

82. *Republican Citizen*, August 30, 1861; VR, August 30, 1861; FE, April 7, May 17, 1865 (CW).

83. SB, May 10, 1865 (PQ).

84. George Elliott, June 24, 1861 (www.soldierstudies.org).

85. S. Millet Thompson, *Thirteenth Regiment New Hampshire Volunteer Infantry* (Boston: Houghton, Mifflin, 1888), 30–1.

86. www.home.valstar.net/~jcraig/bogardus.htm.

87. William Child, *History of the 5th Regiment N. H. Volunteers* (Bristol, NH: Musgrove, 1893), 109.

88. Cowart Family Papers, Monmouth County Historical Society Assn. (MON).

89. Survivors' Association, *A History of the 118th Pennsylvania Volunteers* (Philadelphia: J.L. Smith, 1905), 35, 37.

90. Auchmuty, *Letters of Richard Tylden Auchmuty*, 106.

91. Francis H. Buffum, *A Memorial of the Great Rebellion* (Boston: Franklin Press, 1882), 91–2.

92. James Pearre Collection, 1831–1880, Vol. 1 (MdHS).

93. SB, June 7, 1861 (PQ).

94. *OR*, ser. 1, vol. 19, part 2, 474.

95. *South*, May 30, 1861 (MSA).

96. SB, July 27, 16, 17, 1861 (PQ).

97. Engelbrecht, February 11, 1862.

98. Judith Bailey and Robert Cottom, eds., *After Chancellorsville: Letters from the Heart* (Baltimore: Maryland Historical Society, 1998), 6–7.

99. SB, July 16, 1861; September 24, 1861; October 28, 1861 (PQ).

100. SB, August 25, 1864 (PQ); BC, August 25, 1864 (MSA).

101. *South*, May 31, 1861 (MSA).

102. SB, October 14, 1861; November 17, 1864; January 31, 1864 (PQ); VR, July 26, 1861 (CW).

103. Stephen V. Ash, *When the Yankees Came* (Chapel Hill: University of North Carolina Press, 1995), 201.

104. Crystal N. Feimster, "Rape and Justice in the Civil War," Opinionator, *New York Times*, April 25, 2013.

105. SB, March 6, 1862 (PQ); HFTL, December 4, 1861 (CW).

106. George W. Booth, *A Maryland Boy in Lee's Army* (Lincoln: University of Nebraska Press, 2000; original 1898), 129–13.

CHAPTER 4

107. James Davis, ed., *Bully for the Band: The Civil War Letters of Four Brothers* (Jefferson, NC: McFarland, 2012), 175 (MON).

108. SB, March 18, 1863 (PQ).

109. Foote, *Gentlemen and the Roughs*, 30.

110. Wild, *War from the Inside*, 36–7.

111. McClune, *Camp Life*, 25.

112. *Civil War Letters of Henry Ropes: Manuscript, 1859–1863*, Letter, January 3, 1862.

113. Stephen M. Weld, *War Diary and Letters* (Cambridge, MA: Riverside Press, 1912), 262.

114. *Selections from the Letters and Diaries of Brevet & Brigadier General Willoughby* (N.p.: University of the State of NY, 1922), 88–9.

115. James Harvey McGee, *"Back in War Times"—History of the 144th Regiment, NY Volunteer Infantry* (Boure, MD: Heritage Books, 1903), 111– (MON).

116. John D. Bloodgood, *Personal Reminiscences of the War* (New York: Hunt and Eaton, 1893), 129.

117. George Thomas Stevens, *Three Years in the Sixth Corps* (New York: D. Van Nostrand, 1870), 240.

118. Whitelaw Reid, *Cincinnati Gazette*, in Frederic Shriver Klein, *Just South of Gettysburg, Carroll County Maryland in the Civil War* (Maryland: Historical Society of Carroll County, 1963), 129.

119. FE, March 16, 1864; February 3, 1866 (CW).

120. SB, January 1, 1864; October 16, 1862; December 27, 1862 (PQ).

121. BC, September 28, 1864 (MSA).

122. Keller, *Events of the Civil War*, 342.

123. Charles H. Russell Letters, Letter to Ward H. Lamon, May 12, 1862 (WB).

124. Osceola Lewis, *History of the 138th Regiment, Pennsylvania Volunteer Infantry* (Norristown, PA: Wills, Iredell & Jenkins, 1866), 22–3.

125. *OR*, ser. 1, vol. 43, part 2, 294.

126. SB, March 27, 1864; June 18, 1864 (PQ).

127. EG, March 1, 1862 (MSA); SB, April 20, 1865; May 11, 1865 (PQ).

128. SB, May 29, 1865 (PQ).

129. Rev. Alonzo Quint, *The Second Massachusetts Infantry* (Boston, 1867), 90 (MON).

130. SB, April 7, 1864 (PQ); FE, November 26, 1862; May 5, 1863 (CW); BC, August 19, 1864 (MSA); SB, November 14, 1864 (PQ).

131. BC, January 9, 1865 (MSA); SB, May 2, 1864 (PQ); BC, July 28, August 16, August 26, 1864 (MSA); SB, September 14, 1864 (PQ); BC, September 14, 1864 (MSA).

132. BC, January 2, 1865 (MSA).

133. BC, August 31 and 18, 1864 (MSA); SB, July 19, 1864 (PQ).

134. SB, October 6, 1864; October 5 and 8, 1863 (PQ); FE, December 21, 1864; HFTL, January 29, 1862 (CW).

CHAPTER 5

135. J. Harrison Mills, *Chronicles of the 21st Regiment NY State Volunteers* (Buffalo, NY: 21st Regiment Veteran Assn., 1887), 74.

136. FE, August 21, 1861; VR, July 5 and June 28, 1861 (CW).

137. SB, October 24, 1864 (PQ).

138. SB, September 10, 1863; January 30, 1865 (PQ).

139. SB, September 15, 1863; February 27, 1864; July 24, 1863 (PQ).

140. *Baltimore Daily Gazette*, February 27, 1864.

141. SB, February 4, 1863 (PQ).

142. FE, January 15, 1862 (CW).

143. Wild, *War from the Inside*, 71–2.

144. Walcott, *Twenty-First Regiment, Massachusetts Volunteers*, 14.

145. EG, July 26, 1862 (MSA).

146. Christian Fleetwood, *The Negro as Soldier* (Washington, D.C.: Howard University Press, 1895), 6, 9.

147. *Speech of the Hon. Henry May of Maryland, delivered in the House of Representatives, February 3, 1863* (Baltimore, MD: Kelly & Piet, 1863), 7.

148. Speech of Henry Winter Davis in Philadelphia, September 24, 1863; Speech of the Hon. Henry Winter Davis in the House of Representatives, March 22, 1864.

149. Frederick Douglass, "Men of Color, to Arms" and "Why a Colored Man Should Enlist," (LOC).

150. Dr. Alexander T. Augusta, http://encyclopedia.jrank.org/articles/pages/4107/Augusta-Alexander-T-1825-1890.html; Heather M. Butts, *Journal National Medical Assn.* 97 (2005): 107.

151. SB, May 2, 1863 (PQ).

152. Brett W. Spaulding, United States Colored Troops, NPS Presentation (MON).

153. SB, July 28, 1863 (PQ); FE, August 5, 12, 19, 21, 26, 1863 (CW).

154. FE, October 21, 1863; November 4, 1863 (CW).

155. *OR*, ser. 1, vol. 29, part 2, 263–4, 269.

156. U.S. War Department, *Murder of Lieutenant Eben White* (Washington, D.C.: U.S. House, 1874), 5.

157. Haynes, *Minor War History*, 133.

158. Samuel Kramer, *Maryland and the Glorious Old Third* (Washington, D.C.: T.J. Brashears, 1882), 28.

159. SB, March 7, 1864 (PQ).

160. FE, December 16, 1863 (CW).

161. Quint, *Second Massachusetts Infantry*, 38.

162. Gould, 107.

163. William Combs, letter to Eliza Doolittle Combs, November 23, 1862 (www.rarebooks.nd.edu).

164. Andrew E. Ford, *Story of the 15th Regiment Massachusetts Volunteer Infantry* (Clinton, MA: W.J. Coulter, 1898), 129.

165. Leverett Bradley, *A Soldier-Boy's Letters* (Boston: private printing, 1905), 34.

166. Lyman Jackman, *The 6th New Hampshire Regiment* (Concord, NH: Republican Assn., 1891), 114–15.

167. Daniel Eldredge, *Third New Hampshire* (Boston: Press of E.B. Stillings, 1893), 37.

168. EG, May 7, 1863 (MSA).

169. Herbert E. Valentine, *Company F, 23rd Massachusetts Volunteers* (Boston: Clark, 1896), 24.

170. Stephen Abbott, *First Regiment New Hampshire Volunteers* (Keene, NH: Sentinel, 1890), 151–3.

171. Buffum, *Memorial of the Great Rebellion*, 347.

172. William Kirkwood Correspondence, 1857–1923, Letter to Mother, January 1,1862 (MdHS).

173. Edwin Moffett, Letter to Father, January 20, 1863 (MdHS).

174. Thomas Monroe, Letter, June 26, 1865 (Hamilton College Digital Collections).

175. Johnson Family Papers, Dr. Thomas Francis Johnson to William, November 4, 1864 (MdHS).

176. John Gibbon Correspondence, Letter to Mr. Latrobe, September 7, 1865 (MdHS).

CHAPTER 6

177. Dr. Samuel Harrison, Journal, 1861–1865, entry for November 26, 1864 (MdHS).

178. Virginia Beauchamp, ed., *Letters and Diaries of Madge Preston* (New Brunswick, NJ: Rutgers Uinversity Press, 1987), 97.

179. Mrs. Benjamin Gwynn Harris Diaries, September 7, 1861 (MdHS).

180. SB, July 29, 1862 (PQ).

181. SB, August 18, 1864 (PQ).

182. Jonathan W. White, "All For a Sword: The Military Treason Trial of Sarah Hutchins," *Prologue Magazine*, Spring 2012 (National Archives).

183. FE, August 3, 1864; VR, August 12, 1864 (CW).

184. SB, July 3, 1863 (PQ).

185. SB, May 8, 1865 (PQ).

186. George C. Gordon, Letter, October 29, 1862 (www.soldierstudies.org).

187. Samuel Hurst, *Journal History of the 73rd Ohio Volunteer Infantry* (Chillicothe, OH: Hurst, 1866), 64.

188. Davenport, *Camp and Life*, 92.

189. SB, June 25, 1863; April 28, 1864 (PQ); FE, July 9, 1862; August 6, 1862 (CW); SB, March 31, 1863 (PQ); FE, August 3, 1864 (CW).

190. BC, April 21 and 24, 1865 (MSA).

191. Sheads and Toomey, *Baltimore During the Civil War*, 98–9.

192. VR, September 4, 1863 (CW); SB, November 30, 1863; February 18, 1864; April 29, 1864; October 6, 1863; July 7, 1863; September 27, 1864 (PQ).

193. Russell, *My Diary North and South*, 376.

194. VR, September 9, 1864 (CW); BC, September 14, 1864 (MSA); SB, October 9, 1863 (PQ).

195. Robert S. Robertson, *Personal Recollections of the War* (Milwaukee, WI: Swain & Tate, 1895), 63.

196. *Civil War Diary of Nathan Parameter* (Frederick, MD: Historical Society of Frederick County), 56; J.D. Chadwick, http://sites.allegheny.edu/civilwarletters; Weld, *War Diary and Letters*, 240.

197. Henry P. Moyer, *History of the 17th Regiment, Pennsylvania Volunteer Cavalry* (Lebanon, PA: Sowers Printing, 1911), 58.

198. SB, April 20, 1863; September 12 and 30, 1863 (PQ); BC, January 16, 1865 (MSA).

199. Joseph Shaw, "Editor Shaw Describes His Arrest," *Western Maryland Democrat*, September 4, 1862, in Klein, *Just South of Gettysburg*, 10–14, 22.

200. *OR*, ser. 1, vol. 37, part 2, 590.

201. Lew Wallace, Headquarters of Middle Department, April 19, 1865, in BC, April 21, 1865 (MSA).

202. *OR*, ser. 1, vol. 19, part 2, 287.

203. SB, September 4, 1862; April 27, 1865 (PQ).

204. SB, August 4, 1863; December 15, 1864 (PQ).

205. John Eager Howard Papers, Elizabeth Howard to Charles Howard, December 28, 1861; Elizabeth Howard to Charles Howard, September 24, 1862 (MdHS).

206. Joshua Webster Hering, *Recollections of My Life*, Vol. 2, 70 (MdHS).

207. Civil War Diary of James Francis Beall (WB).

208. Harrison, July 17 and August 21, 1861 (MdHS).

209. FE, August 13, 1862 (CW).

210. Sterling Papers, Tillie Sterling to A.V. Farquhar, May 30, 1863; Tillie Sterling to A.V. Farquhar, March 18, 1863 (University of Maryland Digital Library).

211. Volunteer Zouave, *A.D. 1862, or How They Act in Baltimore* (Baltimore. MD: Jas. S. Waters, 1862) (MdHS).

212. Daniel Murray Thomas Papers, Daniel Murray Thomas to Sister, May 27, 1861 (MdHS).

Chapter 7

213. Edwin M. Haynes, *A History of the 10th Regiment, Vermont Volunteers* (Rutland, VT: Tuttle Co., 1894), 222.

214. HFTL, September 16, 1863 (CW).

215. Robert Cruikshank Letters, October 12, 1862, www.ehistory.osu.edu/usciv.

216. William Byrnes, Letter to Florence, September 29, 1861, www.soldierstudies.org.

217. John Frederick Roser, Letter to Lucy, July 1864 (MON).

218. Letter to Cousin, August 8, 1864 (MON).

219. Dixon, "Soldiers of the 'Lost Cause,'" 1.

220. SB, October 1, 1863 (PQ).

221. Keller, *Events of the Civil War*, 248.

222. Ann R.L. Schaeffer, "Records of the Past," September 4–23, 1862, (MdHS).

223. *Report of Lewis H. Steiner*, 11.

224. Frederick L. Hitchcock, *War from the Inside* (Philadelphia: J.B. Lippincott, 1904), 49.

225. HFTL, September, 1862; VR, September 20, 1862 (CW).

226. Elisha Hunt Rhodes, *Diary of a Union Soldier*, September 23, 1862, www.norton.com/college/history/archive/resources/documents.

227. Noyes, *Bivouac and the Battlefield*, 237–8.

228. Rhodes, *Diary of a Union Soldier*, October 15, 1862.

229. Josiah Marshall Favill, *Diary of a Young Officer* (Chicago: R.R. Donnelley, 1909), 190.

230. HFTL, August 8, 1863 (CW).

231. Mr. Reinhart Diary, 1854–1880 (MdHS).

232. William Swinton, *History of the 7th Regiment, National Guard, NY* (New York: Fields, 1870), 316.

233. SB, July 1, 1863; June 30, 1863 (PQ).

234. Diary of First Lieutenant Abiel La Forge, U.S. Army Military Institute (MON).

235. Joseph Bilby, "9 July 1864: The 14th New Jersey at the Battle of Monocacy," *Military Images* (May–June, 1980): 9 (MON).

236. Alfred S. Roe, *Personal Narratives: From Monocacy to Danville* (Providence: Soldiers' and Sailors' Historical Society of Rhode Island, 1889), 6.

237. Mary Guinta, ed., *A Civil War Soldier of God and Country: Selected Correspondence of John Rodgers Meigs* (Urbana, IL: UIP, 2006), 234 (MON).

238. John B. Gordon, *Reminiscences of the Civil War* (Dayton, OH: Morningside, 1893), 312.

239. *New York Times*, "Our Baltimore Correspondence," July 13, 1864 and July 15, 1864 (PQ).

240. SB, July 16, 1864 (PQ).

241. BC, July 29, 1864 (MSA).

242. *OR*, ser. 1, vol. 43. part 1, 755.

243. *Alleganian* (Cumberland), August 3 and 10, 1864 (WB).

244. *OR*, ser. 1, vol. 46, 526.

245. Alban Gilpin Thomas Correspondence, Richard Thomas to Brother, October 10, 1864 (MdHS).

Chapter 8

246. C.F. Johnson, *The Long Roll, Being a Journal of the Civil War* (Aurora, IL: Roycrofters, 1911), 193.

247. Warren H. Freeman, Letter to Father, February 9, 1862, www.soldierstudies.org; Noyes, *Bivouac and the Battlefield*, 165.

248. Robert Cruishank Letters, October 12, 1862; Albinus R. Fell, July 8, 1863 (www.soldierstudies.org).

249. Noyes, *Bivouac and the Battlefield*, 155; William Cline Dairy, 25–6, www.soldierstudies.org.

250. Henry W.T. Tisdale, October 29, 1862, www.civilwardiary.net/diary.

251. Daniel Long, *Civil War Diary of Daniel Long, July 18, 1864* (N.p.: Lowell Fry, 2006) (MON).

252. *Civil War Diary of Nathan Parameter*, 37.

253. W.A. Roberts, Letter to Home, October 25, 1862, in *History of the 45th Regiment Pennsylvania*, 50.

254. Survivors' Association, 35.

255. Samuel McClain Papers, June 3, 1864, Center for Archival Collections (www.bgsu.edu).

256. Daniel Preston Adams, September 25, 1862 (Hamilton College Library Digital Collections).

257. Solon A. Rand, Letters, June 19 and 30, 1864, www.soldierstudies.org.

258. John Hoffman, Letter to Wife, August 14, 1864 (MON).

259. E.Y. Goldsborough, *Early's Great Raid* (Frederick, MD: privately published, 1898), 16 (MON).

260. William Kirkwood Correspondence, 1857–1923, Letter to Mother, March 27, 1862(?) (MdHS).

261. Charles H. Kirk, *History of the 15ᵗʰ Pennsylvania Volunteer Cavalry* (Philadelphia, 1906), 59.

262. *OR*, ser. 1, vol. 19, part 2, 266; 44.

263. Edward P. Tobie, *History of the 1ˢᵗ Maine Cavalry* (Boston: Emory & Hughes, 1887), 93–6.

264. Henry N. Blake, *Three Years in the Army of the Potomac* (Boston: Lee & Shepard, 1865), 46.

265. Willard W. Glazier, *Three Years in the Federal Cavalry* (New York: R.B. Ferguson, 1870), 26.

266. Walcott, *Camp Life*, 8; Theodore B. Gates, *The "Ulster Guard"* (New York: B.H. Tyrrel, 1879), 105–6.

267. Charles H. Lynch, *The Civil War Diary* (Hartford, CT: Case, Lockwood, Brainard, 1915), 9.

268. Thompson, *Thirteenth Regiment New Hampshire Volunteer Infantry*, December 4, 1861; Weld, Letter to Father, March 29, 1864.

269. *Selections from the Letters and Diaries of Brevet & Brigadier General Willoughby*, October 24, 1861.

270. Harris H. Beecher, *Record of the 114th Regiment, NYSV* (New York: J.F. Hubbard, 1866), 398.

271. Stephen Minot Wells, *War Diary and Letters* (Cambridge, MA: Riverside Press, 1912), 243.

272. Robert G. Hill, ed., *A Civil War Diary Kept by Josiah Lewis Hill*, July 19, 1864 (MON).

273. John W. Jacques, *Three Years' Campaign of the 9ᵗʰ NYSM* (New York: Hilton & Co., 1885), 39.

274. EG, December 21, 1862 (MSA).

275. Carter, *Four Brothers in Blue*, 331.

276. Johnson, *The Long Roll, Being a Journal of the Civil War*, 188.

277. Walter S. Goss, *History of the 7ᵗʰ Massachusetts Infantry* (Taunton, MA: 1890), 102.

278. Judith Pizarro et al., "Physical and Mental Health Costs of Traumatic Experiences Among Civil War Veterans," *Archives of General Psychiatry* 62, no. 2 (February 2008): 183–200.

279. Harry Kiefer, *Recollections of a Drummer Boy* (Boston: Ticknor, 1889), 24.

280. Hitchcock, *War from the Inside*, 74; Committee of the Regt, *History of the 35ᵗʰ Regt. MV* (Boston: Mills,1884), 56.

Chapter 9

281. Wild, *Memoirs and History*, 122.

282. See Glymph, "Enslaved Women and the Armies of the Civil War," Speech at Vanderbilt University (2011); Downs, *Sick from Freedom*; Oakes, *Destruction of Slavery*.

283. Steve R. Waddell, *U.S. Army Logistics* (N.p.: Greenwood Publishing, 2010).

284. "Voices of the Civil War" (LOC).

285. HTFL, August 6, 1862; VR, June 12, 1863 (CW); SB, March 26 and September 15, 1864 (PQ).

286. "Memorial Day Speech," May 30, 1884, http://people.virginia.edu/~mmdsf/memorial.htm.

Selected Bibliography

*For full information on all sources used, see endnotes.

Online Data Bases

Catoctin Center for Regional Studies. Crossroads of War. http://www. crossroadsofwar.org.

Cornell University Library. *The War of the Rebellion: A Compilation of the Official Records of the Union and Confederate Armies.* http://digital.library.cornell. edu/m/moawar/waro.html.

Internet Archive. An extensive text collection of letters, diaries, memoirs and regimental histories. http://archive.com.

Library of Congress. http://www.loc.gov.

Maryland State Archives. Online collections of early state records, records of the three branches of state government, etc. http://msa.maryland.gov.

ProQuest.com. Historical newspapers.

University of Maryland Digital Library. http://digital.lib.umd.edu.

Western Maryland Historical Library. Contains letters, diaries, photos, newspapers. http://www.whilbr.org.

ARCHIVES

Antietam and Monocacy National Battlefield Archives

Historical Society of Frederick County—see online catalogue

Maryland Historical Society—extensive collections of manuscripts of soldiers and civilians from both sides; rare pamphlets and books; newspapers; photos

Maryland State Archives

SELECTED SECONDARY SOURCES

Ash, Stephen V. *When the Yankees Came.* Chapel Hill: University of North Carolina Press, 1995.

Baker, Jean. *The Politics of Continuity: Maryland Political Parties from 1858 to 1870.* Baltimore, MD: Johns Hopkins University Press, 1973.

Cottom, Robert I., and Mary Ellen Hayward. *Maryland in the Civil War.* Baltimore: Maryland Historical Society, 1994.

Ernst, Kathleen E. *Too Afraid to Cry: Maryland Civilians in the Civil War.* Mechanicsburg, PA: Stackpole Books, 1999.

Fields, Barbara Jeanne. *Slavery and Freedom on the Middle Ground: Maryland during the Nineteenth Century.* New Haven, CT: Yale University Press, 1985.

Foote, Lorien. *The Gentleman and the Roughs: Violence, Honor and Manhood in the Union Army*. New York: New York University Press, 2010.

Gordon, Paul, and Rita Gordon. *Frederick County, Maryland: Never the Like Again*. Frederick, MD: self-published, 1995.

Grimsley, Mark. *The Hard Hand of War*. New York: Cambridge University Press, 1995.

Keller, S. Roger, ed. *Crossroads of War: Frederick County, Maryland in the Civil War*. Shippensburg, PA: Burd Street Press, 1997.

———. *Events of the Civil War in Washington County Maryland*. Shippensburg, PA: Burd Street Press, 1995.

Klein, Frederick Shriver, ed. *Just South of Gettysburg*. Maryland: Historical Society of Carroll County, 1963.

Manakee, Harold. *Maryland in the Civil War*. Baltimore: Maryland Historical Society, 1961.

Maryland State Archives and University of Maryland. *Guide to the History of Slavery in Maryland*. N.p., 2007.

Mills, Eric. *Chesapeake Bay in the Civil War*. Centreville, MD: Tidewater Publishers, 1996.

Mitchell, Charles T. *Maryland Voices of the Civil War*. Baltimore, MD: Johns Hopkins University Press, 2007.

Phillips, Christopher. *Freedom's Port: The African American Community of Baltimore, 1790–1860*. Urbana: University of Illinois Press, 1997.

Ramold, Steven J. *Baring the Iron Hand: Discipline in the Union Army*. DeKalb: Northern Illinois Press, 2010.

Ruffner, Kevin Conley. *Maryland's Blue and Gray*. Baton Rouge: Louisiana State University Press, 1997.

Sheads, Scott Sumpter, and Daniel Toomey. *Baltimore During the Civil War*. Linthicum, MD: Toomey Press, 1997.

Toomey, Daniel. *The Civil War in Maryland*. Linthicum, MD: Toomey Press, 1983.

Whitman, T. Stephen. *Challenging Slavery in the Chesapeake*. Baltimore: Maryland Historical Society, 2007.

Wiley, Bell Irvin. *The Life of Billy Yank: The Common Soldier of the Union*. Baton Rouge: Louisiana State University Press, 1951. Reprint, 1971.

Index

About the Author

C laudia Floyd is a retired professor
of history at Stevenson University
in the Baltimore area. She has degrees
from Carlow University, Duquesne
University, Johns Hopkins University
and the University of Maryland–
Baltimore County. At Stevenson, she
taught a variety of courses including
Women's History and the Civil War.
Currently, Claudia volunteers at both
Monocacy National Battlefield and Soldiers Delight Natural Environment
Area. She is also an active member of the Society of Women and the Civil
War. She is the author of *Maryland Women in the Civil War: Unionists, Rebels,
Slaves & Spies* (Charleston, SC: The History Press, 2013).